Heineken WORLD OF GOLF 94

Edited by Nick Edmund

First published 1994

This edition produced for
The Book People Ltd
Guardian House,
Borough Road
Godalming,
Surrey
GU7 2AE

A CIP catalogue record for this book is available from the British Library
ISBN 1 85613 845 3

Designed by Rob Kelland at Allsport
Typeset in Gill and Joanna
Origination by DRS, London
Printed by Cronion SA, Barcelona

PHOTOGRAPHIC CREDITS

Dave Cannon/Allsport: front cover, back cover (inset top and bottom), 3, 4, 5, 12, 15 (top), 16 (all), 18, 19, 20 (bottom left and right), 24, 25, 26, 27, 28, 29, 30, 31 (both), 33, 34, 39, 41, 43 (bottom), 45, 48, 50, 53, 54 (right), 55, 57 (top left and bottom left), 59, 64, 65, 67, 69 (bottom), 70 (both), 71, 74, 76, 78, 80 (right), 81 (both), 82 (right), 88, 93 (both), 94, 96, 97, 98, 99, 100, 102, 103, 108 (both), 109 (both), 110, 111, 115, 124 (both), 125, 129 (left), 136, 138, (bottom), 139 (left), 147, 151, 152 (both), 170, 171 (left), 173, 174, 177, 178 (both), 183, 185, 186, 187, 188, 190, 193, 194, 195, 196, 198, 199, 202, 204, 207, 210, 213 (top), 217, 218, 220 (top), 221 (both), 222; **Allsport:** 8, 44, 90, 106 (right), 128, 130 (bottom), 139 (right), 181 (top), 184 (right), 205 (bottom), 208, 213 (bottom), 214; **Klaus Andersen/Allsport USA:** 146; **Shaun Botterill/Allsport:** 176; **Chris Cole/Allsport:** back cover (inset middle), 7, 52, 57 (top left), 58, 82 (left), 84; **Steve Dunn/Allsport USA:** 131, 132, 137 (left), 150, 151 (inset), 154, 191, 192; **John Gichigi/Allsport:** 105, 197, 224; **Matthew Harris/Allsport:** 17; **Michael Hobbs/Allsport:** 23 (inset); **Rusty Jarrett/Allsport:** 10, 11 (inset, top), 66, 69 (top), 91; **Joe Mann/Allsport:** 159, 164 (top), 165, 200 (inset); **Steve Munday/Allsport:** back cover, 13, 14, 20 (top right), 22, 56, 80 (left), 83, 92, 104, 106 (left), 107, 114 (both), 118, 119, 121, 126, 127, 129 (right), 130 (top), 156, 158, 160, 161 (both), 162, 164 (bottom), 166, 184 (left), 203, 209, 212 (bottom), 216, 219; **Gary Newkirk/Allsport USA:** 11 (main), 40, 42, 43 (top), 62, 77, 134, 135, 137 (right), 138 (top), 141, 144, 179, 180 (both), 181 (bottom), 200, 212 (top), 222; **Andy Redington/Allsport:** 57 (bottom right); **Dave Rogers/Allsport:** 79; **Rick Stewart/Allsport USA:** 205 (top); **Anton Want/Allsport:** 106 (centre), 112, 220 (bottom); **Bob Ewell:** 143, 195 (inset); **Bill Fields:** 15 (bottom); **Phil Inglis:** 117; **Matthew Harris:** 11 (inset, middle and bottom), 32, 49 (inset), 54 (left), 122, 149, 168, 171 (right), 172, 201, 206, 223 (both); **Mark Newcombe:** 20 (top right), 53, 192 (inset)

CONTENTS

Heineken
WORLD OF GOLF
Heineken
WORLD OF GOLF
Heineken
WORLD OF GOLF

5

Global Golf

6

1994: A Year to Savour

7

Great Golf Courses of the World

All text by Nick Edmund unless otherwise credited

Foreword

by Peter Alliss

Perhaps I am a little biased, but I suspect many readers share my view that golf is not only the most wonderful of games but that golfers are among the luckiest people alive. Year after year, our royal and ancient game continues to grow in popularity in all four corners of the globe. As a pastime it has plenty going for it; greater affluence and increased leisure time has no doubt helped, but I think there are two things that make golf particularly special.

Firstly, unlike some sports where there is a clearly defined pitch or court, golf is enjoyed in an incredible array of natural arenas (well, perhaps some not quite so natural). Golfers do not run up and down touch lines gasping for breath; we stroll leisurely through avenues of chestnut and pine, through all sorts of breathtaking scenery. Also, there is the extremely high level of sporting behaviour displayed by all of the game's leading practitioners; we can indeed be proud to be golfers.

Just flick through any of the chapters of this 2nd *Heineken World of Golf* and you will see many illustrations to support these contentions.

Last year the Open was staged at Royal St George's and the US Open at Baltusrol; can you imagine two more contrasting types of golf course and in such different settings? Among the five international events of which Heineken is the title sponsor consider the differences between Noordwijkse in Holland (classic links golf amid tumbling dunes); Lake Nona in Florida (where alligators patrol the water hazards) and the Metropolitan Club in Australia (one of the many great sandbelt courses that surround Melbourne).

Then again, as you peruse the pages of this most strikingly colourful book you will see several examples of sportsmanship and friendly rivalry. The 30th Ryder Cup at The Belfry is an outstanding illustration of a sport being played at the highest level in a splendid spirit; during The Masters at Augusta Chip Beck and Bernhard Langer conversed much during their final round even though at an early stage it developed into a tense head to head type battle. Payne Stewart lost graciously to Lee Janzen at the US Open and Greg Norman showed enormous dignity in the way he handled his second heartbreak at Inverness when he was defeated in a sudden death play-off for the USPGA title by Paul Azinger. Late in the year at the Heineken World Cup – an event founded specifically 'for the furtherance of good fellowship among the (golfing) nations of the world', those watching were treated to a final day fourball comprising the Americans Fred Couples and Davis Love and Mark McNulty and Nick Price from Zimbabwe; they were playing for very high stakes – a duel in the Florida sun – but smiles and courtesy reigned; indeed no sport could wish for four finer ambassadors.

Welcome to this wonderful world of golf.

Peter Alliss · *January 1994*

INTRODUCTION

by Nick Edmund

Great White Sharks and Golden Bears: golf is a strange game. It is also, for the reasons Peter Alliss explains in his foreword, a wonderful game and the purpose of this book is to explore and record some of this wonder.

The *Heineken World of Golf* is a yearbook but, as its title suggests, our intention is to celebrate the international flavour of the game as well as its immediate history.

This second edition seeks to relive the achievements and great golfing moments of 1993 and looks forward to all the major events of 1994. It will guide the reader from Sandwich to Sun City and from the depths of Rae's Creek to the shores of Lake Nona; from Europe to America and from Australia to Japan. Its content isn't limited to detailing men's professional golf, as the women's game, amateur golf and senior golf are also covered in some detail.

A wealth of striking photography appears throughout the book and it is hoped that there is a nice balance in the text between facts and figures, comment and analysis.

For easy reference, the contents have been divided into seven chapters. The first of these, '1993: A Year to Remember' offers a general review of some of the highlights of the past season. It is followed in Chapter Two by a detailed look at how the Masters at Augusta, the US Open at Baltusrol, The Open Championship at Sandwich (a triumph for The Great White Shark) and the USPGA at Inverness were won and lost.

After 'The Majors' comes 'The Ryder Cup', and the story of how Tom Watson's team travelled to Europe and returned from three thrilling days at The Belfry still carrying the famous trophy.

From transatlantic rivalry we move on to 'multinational golf' and a chapter on the Heineken World Cup. The format for this event may be very different from the Ryder Cup but it is a tale with similar themes, namely successful defending and American glory, and its heroes, the most perfectly matched pair in golf – Couples and Love.

Chapter Five is titled 'Global Golf' and is the largest in the book. This is where we journey from continent to continent, reviewing all the major Tours and tournaments around the world. Effectively, this chapter has six sections: a comprehensive review of the European scene is followed by golf in America and again, it is difficult not to comment on the irony of a situation where the leading moneywinner on the PGA Tour is a man named Price and the top performer on the LPGA Tour is a woman called King; Australia comes next, then Japan and the Rest of the World, followed by Senior Golf (a triumph for the Golden Bear) and Amateur Golf.

The penultimate chapter in the book, '1994: A Year to Savour' is where we look ahead and preview all this season's big events. It is a year that promises much, particularly with a US Open at Oakmont and an Open Championship at Turnberry.

Finally there is our 'Great Golf Courses of the World' chapter which, as we explained in the first edition of this book, appears for no

other purpose than to show off some of the game's finest and most unusual playgrounds.

As editor of the *Heineken World of Golf*, I would like to express my sincere thanks to those people without whose support and encouragement a second edition would never have materialised. I thank all the contributing journalists for their fine commentaries and previews, and the many talented photographers, especially David Cannon of Allsport who is the book's principal photographer. I'm sure you'll agree that this edition has been very attractively produced and credit for this must go to the designer, Rob Kelland. It has also been put together remarkably quickly, and without the help of Julie Kay and Andrew Redington at Allsport, not to mention our super-efficient publishers, half of the contents might still be on my dining room table – as well as scattered across the living room floor. A massive thank you also, then, to my wife Teresa. And finally, of course, a big thank you to our generous sponsor, Heineken.

Cheers to all of them... and cheers to you. Good golfing in '94!

NICK EDMUND · *January 1994*

1

1993
A Year to Remember

1993 Highlights and Reflections

It could have been Bernard Gallacher on this page, holding aloft the famous Ryder Cup trophy. Not should have been – but could have been. And if the wheel of fortune had turned just a fraction further in their favour, the players opposite wouldn't be looking quite so distressed. If 1993 demonstrated one thing above all others it was that the margins between success and failure in golf are very fine indeed.

All it needed was for one more European birdie putt to disappear into its cup and Nick Faldo and Paul Azinger would have been playing for more than just personal pride at the conclusion of their Singles match at The Belfry. A few seconds of nervous indecision, we are told, caused Dan Forsman to hit his tee shot into Rae's Creek at the Masters. Had he found the sanctuary of the 12th green in that final round, would Bernhard Langer still have cruised to victory? What if Nick Faldo could have taken one stroke less on the front nine at Royal St George's; might Greg Norman have succumbed to intense pressure from the defending champion? Come to think of it, imagine the scenes and possible repercussions if Faldo's tee shot on the par three 11th had jumped into the hole after hitting the flag full on – holes-in-one at both the Open and the Ryder Cup! And finally, does anybody know how Greg Norman's ball avoided dropping, not once, but twice at the 18th hole on that remarkable Sunday afternoon at Inverness? It was as if the hole had been covered with clingfilm.

Two Majors for The Shark last year and we wouldn't have to debate the identity of 1993's 'player of the year'. As things stand, however, was it Greg Norman who won on three

(Opposite) a triumphant Tom Watson. (Above) 'Stressed? Take up golf' they urged, 'It'll calm the nerves'

continents, or was it Nick Price who won on six occasions?

It has been claimed that 1993 saw a significant shift in golf's so-called 'balance of power'. The contention is that the 'power' has swung away from Europe in favour of the United States and is based on the fact that all of the major international team trophies were won last year by teams from America. But surely, if there was any shift it wasn't of a transatlantic nature, rather it was from the Northern Hemisphere to the Southern Hemisphere (a 'downwardly mobile' shift!)

John Daly drives at St Andrews; (right) Fred Couples plays from 'the beach' at Lake Nona

Tom Watson's 'Twelve good men and true' won the Ryder Cup in September; Fred Couples, John Daly and Payne Stewart won the Alfred Dunhill Cup at St Andrews in October and in November, Fred Couples and Davis Love successfully defended the Heineken World Cup at Lake Nona in Florida. Late in the year, at important individual tournaments, American golfers triumphed in the Toyota World Matchplay Championship (Corey Pavin), the Heineken Australian Open (Brad Faxon) and the Johnnie Walker World Championship (Larry Mize). Each of these events was won deservedly – no question about that – but in the Major championships, and more especially on their home Tour, American golfers certainly didn't dominate.

Three of the year's four Grandslam events are always staged in America. In 1993 US golfers won two of these four championships; one was claimed by a European and one by an

Australian. Only the Masters was won by more than two strokes and, as all the golfing world should know, the destination of the famous Green Jacket is never determined until every challenger has negotiated Amen Corner, Augusta's notorious 11th, 12th and 13th holes. The only 'all American affair' was the US Open – so, what's new? On the US PGA Tour the majority of the more prestigious tournaments were won by overseas players. In addition to Langer's Masters victory, Nick Price collected both the Players Championship and the Western Open titles; Fulton Allem won the Colonial and World Series events; David Frost won the Canadian Open and Brett Ogle was a winner at Pebble Beach. Perhaps it was the ghost of Uncle Sam who put clingfilm over the 18th hole at Inverness in the USPGA

Revelation or revolution? England's Trish Johnson led the European assault on America's LPGA Tour in 1993

Championship and made Greg Norman bogey four of the last seven holes to lose the Tour Championship at San Francisco.

It has to be good for the world of golf (players and spectators alike) that no one country and no single player dominates the game. In Europe, where Colin Montgomerie overtook Nick Faldo in the final event of the season to become Leading Moneywinner, the 40 Tour events were won by players from 13 different countries. For the first time ever a Swedish and an Italian golfer played in the Ryder Cup. Perhaps the most striking illustration of how the 'rest of the world' has been catching up with the established golfing nations came at St Andrews when the team from Paraguay defeated host nation Scotland in their Alfred Dunhill Cup encounter. Old Tom Morris must have turned in his grave.

The achievements of non-American golfers on the US PGA Tour has already been referred to, but in addition to the European, South African, Zimbabwean and Australian triumphs, 1993 brought a first ever US Tour victory for a Fijian golfer, the highly talented Vijay Singh, and a surprise win for New Zealand's Grant Waite. Southern Hemisphere players finished the season occupying four of the top nine positions on the PGA Money List.

The threat to US hegemony in women's golf has a much more recent history. Prior to Europe's victory in the 1992 Solheim Cup almost all the stars of the LPGA Tour were American. In 1993 women golfers from Europe, fuelled by that famous win at Dalmahoy, went berserk (so to speak). Helen Alfredsson of Sweden claimed a Major championship, England's Trish Johnson won

(Right) Europe's 'shot of the year': Seve Ballesteros contrived to finish his round with a birdie from this perilous position at the European Masters

(Below) America's 'shot of the year': Paul Azinger holed this bunker shot at the final hole to defeat Payne Stewart and win the Memorial Tournament

two events in succession and Laura Davies and Helen Dobson also won. Another English golfer, Suzanne Strudwick was the LPGA Rookie of the Year. The Americans fought back, however, and last year Betsy King became Leading Moneywinner and Patty Sheehan, Brandie Burton and Lauri Merten triumphed in the remaining LPGA Majors. Sheehan was also presented with 30 red roses by Tour Commissioner Charles Mechem at the Standard Register Ping tournament when she achieved her 30th Tour victory. The win heralded her entry into one of golf's most exclusive clubs, the LPGA Hall of Fame.

European hazards: England's Peter Baker plays from a cavernous bunker at St Andrews; Sweden's Anders Forsbrand finds deep rough at Noordwijkse and America's Corey Pavin is brought to his knees at Wentworth

The international flavour of winners has even spread to Japan, it would seem. Last year 'Jumbo' Ozaki and Hajime Meshiai battled all year for the number one position on the Order of Merit but no fewer than 12 of the Japanese Tour's 39 events were won by foreign players. Greg Norman was a winner in Japan last year, his victory coming in the Taiheiyo Visa Masters tournament where he finished, as only Greg Norman could finish, scoring one double-bogey and two eagles in his last eight holes!

There was plenty of typical Shark behaviour to enjoy last year but we saw precious little of vintage Ballesteros. Seve suffered what a certain sovereign lady might describe as, an 'annus horribilis' in 1993. There were some magical moments in the Ryder Cup and he also produced 'Europe's shot of the year' (see page 15) but as for his season as a whole, let's

(Left) Japanese evergreen Masashi 'Jumbo' Ozaki. (Opposite) Gary Player wants to check Nick Price's temperature after the Zimbabwean's amazing twelve stroke victory at Sun City last December

just say that he's looking forward to 1994.

It is to The Great White Shark that we must award the accolade, 'greatest round of the year'. If Greg Norman considers his closing 64 in the Open Championship at Royal St George's to be his finest ever 18 holes of golf that's good enough for us. There were, of course, many other great rounds in 1993 and among the best (in that they each came in the final round by a tournament winner) we might mention the extraordinary 63 by Peter Baker in the Dunhill British Masters at Woburn, the 62 by Fulton Allem that destroyed the field at Firestone in The World Series and the 64 by Ian Baker-Finch (including an outward nine of 29) that enabled him to overcome a nine shot deficit in the Australian PGA Championship.

Having discussed 'the shot of the year' and 'the round of the year'; what about 'the finest four-round performance of 1993'? The answer to this will possibly also settle our 'player of the year' debate and probably depends on how much emphasis is placed upon the greater status of Major championships. We suggest that the two leading contenders are Greg Norman's 13 under par, 66-68-69-64 to win the Open Championship (by two strokes from Nick Faldo) and Nick Price's 24 under par, 67-66-66-65 to win the Sun City Million Dollar Challenge (by 12 shots from Mark McNulty). In view of his comments at Sandwich, we can safely assume that Gene Sarazen would vote for Greg Norman and, if the picture above is anything to go by, Gary Player might give his decision in favour of Nick Price. And you... how would you cast your vote?

THE SONY RANKINGS

31ST · DECEMBER · 1993

Position	Player	Circuit	Points
1	Nick Faldo	Eur	20.65
2	Greg Norman	ANZ	18.79
3	Bernhard Langer	Eur	17.19
4	Nick Price	Afr	15.89
5	Fred Couples	USA	14.93
6	Paul Azinger	USA	14.59
7	Ian Woosnam	Eur	11.41
8	Tom Kite	USA	10.07
9	Davis Love III	USA	9.61
10	Corey Pavin	USA	9.59
11	David Frost	Afr	9.45
12	Masashi Ozaki	Jpn	9.28
13	Payne Stewart	USA	9.23
14	Colin Montgomerie	Eur	9.05
15	José-Maria Olazabal	Eur	8.91
16	Vijay Singh	Asa	8.73
17	Mark McNulty	Afr	8.33
18	John Cook	USA	8.15
19	Steve Elkington	ANZ	7.45
20	Ernie Els	Afr	6.79
21	Larry Mize	USA	6.76
22	Lee Janzen	USA	6.72
23	Chip Beck	USA	6.22
24	Raymond Floyd	USA	6.20
25	Seve Ballesteros	Eur	6.16
26	Tom Watson	USA	6.12
27	Peter Senior	ANZ	5.98
28	Mark O'Meara	USA	5.92
29	Scott Simpson	USA	5.81
30	Tony Johnstone	Afr	5.74
31	Gordon Brand Jnr	Eur	5.71
32	Frank Nobilo	ANZ	5.67
33	Costantino Rocca	Eur	5.62
34	Jim Gallagher Jnr	USA	5.60
35	Mark James	Eur	5.55
36	Brad Faxon	USA	5.49
37	Sam Torrance	Eur	5.49
38	Barry Lane	Eur	5.48
39	David Edwards	USA	5.46
40	Rodger Davis	ANZ	5.43
41	Rocco Mediate	USA	5.41
42	Bruce Lietzke	USA	5.30
43	David Gilford	Eur	5.23
44	Craig Parry	ANZ	5.21
45	Ronan Rafferty	Eur	5.19
46	Fuzzy Zoeller	USA	5.10
47	Phil Mickelson	USA	5.06
48	Tom Lehman	USA	4.95
49	Craig Stadler	USA	4.93
50	Jeff Maggert	USA	4.93
51	Jay Haas	USA	4.87
52	Dan Forsman	USA	4.80
53	Tsuneyuki Nakajima	Jpn	4.78
54	Wayne Westner	Afr	4.76
55	Fulton Allem	Afr	4.67
56	Mark Calcavecchia	USA	4.65
57	Sandy Lyle	Eur	4.64
58	Darren Clarke	Eur	4.64
59	Anders Forsbrand	Eur	4.64
60	Steven Richardson	Eur	4.60
61	Nolan Henke	USA	4.59
62	Gil Morgan	USA	4.59
63	Joakim Haeggman	Eur	4.50
64	Ben Crenshaw	USA	4.48
65	Eduardo Romero	SAm	4.42
66	Ian Baker-Finch	ANZ	4.38
67	Rick Fehr	USA	4.29
68	John Huston	USA	4.20
69	David Feherty	Eur	4.16
70	Peter Baker	Eur	4.12

Nick Faldo retained his Number One position throughout 1993. (Opposite) Australia's Robert Allenby is tipped to make an impact on the world stage in 1994

Maxfli

2

The Majors

THE MASTERS
THE US OPEN
THE OPEN CHAMPIONSHIP
THE USPGA

The Masters

THE MASTERS

ROLL · OF · HONOUR

Larry Mize wins in 1987

1934	Horton Smith
1935	* Gene Sarazen
1936	Horton Smith
1937	Byron Nelson
1938	Henry Picard
1939	Ralph Guldahl
1940	Jimmy Demaret
1941	Craig Wood
1942	* Byron Nelson
1943-5	No championships played
1946	Herman Keiser
1947	Jimmy Demaret
1948	Claude Harmon
1949	Sam Snead
1950	Jimmy Demaret
1951	Ben Hogan
1952	Sam Snead
1953	Ben Hogan
1954	* Sam Snead
1955	Cary Middlecoff
1956	Jack Burke
1957	Doug Ford
1958	Arnold Palmer
1959	Art Wall
1960	Arnold Palmer
1961	Gary Player
1962	* Arnold Palmer
1963	Jack Nicklaus
1964	Arnold Palmer
1965	Jack Nicklaus
1966	* Jack Nicklaus
1967	Gay Brewer
1968	Bob Goalby
1969	George Archer
1970	* Billy Casper
1971	Charles Coody
1972	Jack Nicklaus
1973	Tommy Aaron
1974	Gary Player
1975	Jack Nicklaus
1976	Ray Floyd
1977	Tom Watson
1978	Gary Player
1979	* Fuzzy Zoeller
1980	Seve Ballesteros
1981	Tom Watson
1982	* Craig Stadler
1983	Seve Ballesteros
1984	Ben Crenshaw
1985	Bernhard Langer
1986	Jack Nicklaus
1987	* Larry Mize
1988	Sandy Lyle
1989	* Nick Faldo
1990	* Nick Faldo
1991	Ian Woosnam
1992	Fred Couples
1993	Bernhard Langer

* Winner in play-off.

· HIGHLIGHTS ·

Most wins:
6 Jack Nicklaus
4 Arnold Palmer

Most times runner-up:
4 Ben Hogan
Tom Weiskopf
Jack Nicklaus

Biggest margin of victory:
9 Jack Nicklaus (1965)

Lowest winning total:
271 Jack Nicklaus (1965)
Ray Floyd (1976)

Lowest single round:
63 Nick Price (1986)

Record front nine:
30 Johnny Miller (1975)
Greg Norman (1988)

Record back nine:
29 Mark Calcavecchia (1992)

Lowest final round by winner:
64 Gary Player (1978)

Oldest champion:
Jack Nicklaus, aged 46 (1986)

Youngest champion:
Severiano Ballesteros, aged 23 (1980)

THE 1993 MASTERS

April and Augusta. The 57th Masters would open with three sparkling birdies from the irrepressible Arnold Palmer and would close with a majestic eagle from the indomitable Bernhard Langer. Diamonds and steel.

It was Easter weekend and the stage was set. The dogwoods and azaleas were out in full force, and so too, for a marvellous moment anyway, was 'Arnie's Army'. On Masters Thursday the 63 year-old four-time champion began his round birdie-birdie-birdie – just as he always used to (so legend has it). Of course these days Arnie cannot keep it going, but the presence, indeed parading of his name on all the leaderboards seemed to inspire his old adversaries: evergreen Gary Player compiled a solid one under par 71; Ray Floyd had a fine 68 while Jack Nicklaus, for so long Palmer's greatest rival, returned a vintage 67. Yes, Thursday definitely belonged to the old warriors.

Payne Stewart: all dressed up but no place to go

Nicklaus' five under par score – his lowest since that unforgettable Sunday in 1986 – was good enough for a share of the first round lead with fellow Americans, Corey Pavin, Larry Mize, Tom Lehman and Lee Janzen. So it wasn't just seniors' day then; it was also America's. Of the 13 players who broke 70 on the opening day only two such scores were achieved by overseas challengers, namely Bernhard Langer (68) and Craig Parry (69). This slow start from the non-American contingent was a little surprising since the three pre-tournament favourites were England's Nick Faldo, Greg Norman of Australia and the Zimbabwean Nick Price. Faldo and Price were not too far off the early pace, after rounds of 71 and 72 respectively (although they would both meet with disaster the following day), but Greg Norman struggled to a two over par 74, seven strokes behind the leading quintet.

The weather in Georgia is rather more predictable than it is in, say, London and when the local forecasters reckoned there was a 100% chance of precipitation on Friday you knew for sure that at some point it was going to rain (as Londoners say) like cats and dogs. Well, before the bad weather came Nick Price played some very bad golf; 81 strokes he took, including a quadruple bogey eight at the 14th. His score was the third worst of the entire field and exactly a shot per hole more than when he set his course record 63 in 1986. A rare weekend off, then, for Nick Price. For 11

Legends in their own lifetime: Seve Ballesteros, champion in 1980 and 1983 and Arnold Palmer, champion in 1958, 1960, 1962 and 1964 were paired together on Friday

Nick Faldo's chances of winning a third Masters title vanished in Rae's Creek

holes on Friday the English Nick played beautifully from tee to green and despite being unable to hole a putt of any sizeable length, was one under par as he stood on the tee of the infamous par three 12th. Amazingly, Faldo did a Price (or with hindsight perhaps one should say, a Forsman) as he too contrived to register a quadruple bogey – his ball twice rolling agonisingly into Rae's Creek. Amen. The world number one did manage to avoid the half-way cut but in '10 minutes of madness' his hopes of a third Masters Green Jacket had effectively drowned.

It wasn't all doom and gloom though for the international brigade on Good Friday. Greg Norman finally found some form on the back nine, coming home in 32 with four successive birdies from the 12th, while Seve Ballesteros did even better. It was the Spaniard's 36th birthday and, as if by way of a special treat, he was paired with Arnold Palmer in the second round. (If only Walter Hagen could have been there too – we might have filmed 'Swashbucklers Through the Ages'!) But this time Palmer couldn't rise to the occasion, and nor could Seve, or so it seemed, as they walked to the 10th tee both five over par for the tournament.

Now Seve's golf, of course, is about as predictable as the aforementioned London weather and producing a series of astonishing strokes he proceeded to birdie the 11th, 12th, 13th, 15th and 16th; at both short holes, the 12th and 16th he came within inches of holing his tee shot and at the 18th he missed a putt of four feet for an inward nine of 30. It was scintillating stuff but even at level par the champion of 1980 and 1983 was still seven shots behind the tournament leader.

With one significant exception American golfers continued to monopolise the 1993 Masters. It wasn't the more celebrated home players, such as Couples (the defending champion) or Stewart, Azinger and Kite – indeed the later two missed the cut – but the likes of Jeff Maggert, Russ Cochran and Dan Forsman. Maggert had surged to the front courtesy of a birdie at the 12th and an eagle at the 15th.

The leaderboard wasn't entirely clear on Friday evening, however, for the promised heavy rain made its appearance and prevented 10 players from completing their rounds. Two of the 'old warriors', Nicklaus and Floyd, were still in the thick of things, and so too, rather

As happy as Larry: Langer (above) does a Mize by chipping-in at the 11th on Saturday. John Daly made a late bid for glory on Sunday afternoon (right)

ominously, was Bernhard Langer. With two holes of his second round to play before the enforced early stoppage the German was just one stroke behind Maggert at six under and was playing with the confidence of a man completely in control of his swing.

The calamities of Faldo and Price; Maggert leading the Masters; the brilliance of Ballesteros and the deluge all vied as big story of the day on Friday but Saturday was very different. Saturday belonged entirely to 35 year-old Langer. If there was a supporting role in the third round then it was played by a stiff breeze. Nobody could claim that the famous Augusta pines were swaying in the wind but according to the players there was a lot of 'swirling and gusting' going on.

If most of the field appeared confused, Langer seemed utterly cocooned. Seventy-two was a good score on Saturday: among the

Americans who could be considered still in contention, only Chip Beck achieved this score; Jeff Maggert crashed to a 75. In fact, only three players bettered 71 all day. After finishing his second round with two pars, Langer scored a 69 in his third round. 'That was one of the finest performances of my career', he declared. The highlight, and most significant moment of the afternoon came with his superb chip-in at the 11th from close was Langer's to win? Perhaps the extraordinary run of European successes in Bobby Jones' great tournament had upset the local journalists. In any event Jones would have greatly admired the way that Langer went out and won the 57th Masters.

Langer ultimately turned his four stroke lead into a four shot winning margin but no final round at Augusta is ever without incident. There were, of course, the last day

A cool champion, Langer (left) kept his head on the back nine when all about were losing their's. The agonies of Amen Corner: Dan Forsman (above left) on his way to a seven at the 12th; Seve Ballesteros (above right) heading for a seven at the 15th

to the spot where Larry Mize broke Greg Norman's heart in 1987.

From being one behind at the start of the day Langer was now four ahead of the field. He stood on nine under par (207); Beck and Forsman were on 211 and Cochran, Maggert, Elkington and Wadkins were a further shot back on 212.

'It's Langer's to lose' was the rather ill-conceived and inappropriate headline in Sunday morning's Augusta Chronicle. Surely it charges, though not for once from Greg Norman – six shots behind Langer at the start of the day. To the galleries' immense delight 'Long' John Daly had a go. With the help of an eagle at the 2nd, where he almost holed his seven-iron second shot, he moved to six under par after 13 holes but then ran out of steam. 'Swashbuckling Seve' pitched-in for a birdie at the 14th to go to five under but then promptly dumped his 80-yards wedge shot into Rae's Creek at the 15th.

Easter parade. A warm reception for Langer as he approaches the final green on Sunday

The more serious threats came from Langer's playing partner, Chip Beck and from Dan Forsman. After nine holes Forsman had advanced to within a stroke of Langer and Beck was just two behind. What occurred over the next few holes has become part of Masters history. As always, history can be interpreted and judged in diverse ways. Will the abiding memory be of Forsman's demise at the 12th? For sure, he will never forget how with the golfing world watching his every move he twice hit his ball into Rae's Creek. Or should we debate the wisdom of Chip Beck's decision not to 'go for broke' at the 15th – his last realistic chance of catching the German? Maybe, but why dwell on the negative? Three shots to the 13th hole really decided the outcome of the 1993 Masters: a brave and perfectly shaped tee shot that finished in the centre-left of the fairway; a drilled three-iron that covered the flag and a 20 foot eagle putt which, from the moment it left Langer's putter, was destined for the bottom of the cup. Pure steel.

1993 Masters

FINAL · SCORES

Bernhard Langer receives his second Masters Green Jacket from the 1992 champion, Fred Couples

B Langer	**68**	**70**	**69**	**70**	**277**	**$306,000**
C Beck	72	67	72	70	281	183,600
T Lehman	67	75	73	68	283	81,600
J Daly	70	71	73	69	283	81,600
S Elkington	71	70	71	71	283	81,600
L Wadkins	69	72	71	71	283	81,600
J-M Olazabal	70	72	74	68	284	54,850
D Forsman	69	69	73	73	284	54,850
P Stewart	74	70	72	69	285	47,600
B Faxon	71	70	72	72	285	47,600
A Forsbrand	71	74	75	66	286	34,850
S Ballesteros	74	70	71	71	286	34,850
C Pavin	67	75	73	71	286	34,850
S Simpson	72	71	71	72	286	34,850
R Floyd	68	71	74	73	286	34,850
F Zoeller	75	67	71	73	286	34,850
I Woosnam	71	74	73	69	287	24,650
M Calcavecchia	71	70	74	72	287	24,650
H Twitty	70	71	73	73	287	24,650
J Sluman	71	72	71	73	287	24,650
M O'Meara	75	69	73	71	288	17,000
F Couples	72	70	74	72	288	17,000
L Mize	67	74	74	73	288	17,000
S Lyle	73	71	71	73	288	17,000
J Maggert	70	67	75	76	288	17,000
R Cochran	70	69	73	76	288	17,000
J Nicklaus	67	75	76	71	289	12,350
H Irwin	74	69	74	72	289	12,350
J Sindelar	72	69	76	72	289	12,350
N Henke	76	69	71	73	289	12,350
B Lietzke	74	71	71	74	290	10,533
A Magee	75	69	70	76	290	10,533
G Norman	74	68	71	77	290	10,533
G Sauers	74	71	75	71	291	8,975
B Gilder	69	76	75	71	291	8,975
P Mickelson	72	71	75	73	291	8,975
C Stadler	73	74	69	75	291	8,975
J Haas	70	73	75	74	292	8,000
N Faldo	71	76	79	67	293	6,817
T Schulz	69	76	76	72	293	6,817
D Waldorf	72	75	73	73	293	6,817
K Clearwater	74	70	75	74	293	6,817
J Cook	76	67	75	75	293	6,817
L Janzen	67	73	76	77	293	6,817
M Ozaki	75	71	77	71	294	4,940
N Ozaki	74	70	78	72	294	4,940
T Watson	71	75	73	75	294	4,940
J D Blake	71	74	73	76	294	4,940
C Parry	69	72	75	78	294	4,940
G Morgan	72	74	72	77	295	4,250
B Ogle	70	74	71	80	295	4,250
D Peoples	71	73	78	74	296	4,050
C Montgomerie	71	72	78	75	296	4,050
I Baker-Finch	73	72	73	80	298	3,900
D Edwards	73	73	76	76	298	3,900
D Love III	73	72	76	77	298	3,900
C Coody	74	72	75	78	299	3,800
G Hallberg	72	74	78	75	299	3,800
J Huston	68	74	84	75	301	3,800
G Player	71	76	75	80	302	3,700
B Andrade	73	74	80	76	303	3,700

The Feel of the Masters, the Touch of a Master

A Commentary by Dermot Gilleece

More than 50 years before the great Bobby Jones was born, the owner of an indigo plantation could view from his secluded home, a shadowy canopy of white magnolia blossoms, stretching for 300 yards to the main road beyond. Magnolia Lane has since become the most celebrated driveway in golf, capturing, as one American writer described it, all the tragedies there ever were in the Old South and all the tranquillity there ever would be.

It is the driveway to Augusta National Golf Club, where Jones created a home for the Masters Tournament, which had its inaugural staging in 1934. Since then, it has attained a reverence almost unmatched in sport, a mystique which in many respects is difficult to fathom against the background of such a relatively short history.

Captives of Augusta National's fascinating, almost fabulous appeal, will talk of those magnolia trees as a metaphor for everything about the Masters. The unstudied beauty of the manner in which the flowers frame the course; of the understated elegance of the place and the wealth of tradition that has been packed into its 59-year existence.

And through another metaphor in which the enormous historical impact of the American Civil War is recalled, they will talk of each of the 18 golf holes as a monument to a great battle – in certain cases a tragic defeat for such as Scott Hoch, Seve Ballesteros, Greg Norman and, most recently, Dan Forsman in 1993. Or there could be the triumphs of Jack Nicklaus, Sandy Lyle, Nick Faldo, Larry Mize and Bernhard Langer. The Masters has it all.

The most treacherous element of the majestic course is unquestionably its greens, which were once described by the great Henry Cotton as individual torture arenas. He went on to explain: 'I have never seen holes cut in the incredible spots that they are for the Masters; anywhere but the centre of the green – behind bunkers, on the edge of water hazards and on steep slopes. Or all three! I do not remember ever coming across greens with such slopes on them. Yet, somehow, the winners manage.'

Cotton penned those words at a time when Augusta had rye-grass greens. Given the steep slopes, they were unquestionably quick. But they never reached the pace of the current greens which, in a major gamble, were re-sown with bent grass during the late 1970s. The gamble hinged on the fact that only one other course in the American South had successfully changed to bent, so there was no guarantee that it could survive Georgia's hostile climate of intense heat and long periods without rain.

When considering the current speed of the greens, one must also take into account the dramatic changes that have taken place in the quality of mowing machines. Indeed it is estimated that championship greens in the US are now as much as 70 per cent faster than when Ben Hogan was in his prime. This is reflected in aggregate scores for the Masters over the last 15 years.

Where records are being broken in all of the other 'Majors', reflecting an ongoing rise in the overall standard of play, nobody in recent years has come close to matching the record aggregate of 271 for Augusta, set by Jack Nicklaus in 1965 and equalled by

Raymond Floyd in 1976, again on the old, rye-grass greens.

Often, it takes no more than the gentlest touch of a putter to send the ball careering down one of Augusta's treacherous slopes, yards past the target. It is a situation which prompted me to ask Nicklaus if putting of that nature actually constitutes a golfing stroke in the strict sense of the term. Typically, his answer was unequivocal. 'Certainly,' he replied. 'Putting should be as much a test of nerve as of skill.'

Three years before winning the Masters for the first time, Bernhard Langer was involved in a harrowing climax to the 1982 British PGA Championship at Hillside. Here was a classic case of an important tournament being lost rather than won. Even moderate putting by Langer over the closing holes would have given him the title but, crippled by the dreaded yips, he contrived to present it to an equally struggling Tony Jacklin in a play-off.

From his earliest years as a professional, putting had always been a major flaw in the German's game. Yet he had borne such problems with a patient shrug, conquering his weakness through remarkable mental strength. So it was that in 1985 at Augusta National, he never allowed the horror of that Hillside experience to jeopardise his prospects of becoming only the third foreign player to don the coveted green jacket.

The tournament had seemed destined for Curtis Strange who, after a wretched opening round of 80, recovered to a 65 on Friday, followed by a 68 on Saturday. And with only six holes of the final round to play, Strange led the field by three strokes, apparently destined to complete one of the great comebacks in history.

Over those fateful finishing holes, however, the American's nerve failed him. Bogeys at the 13th, 15th and 18th holes wrecked his victory chance and it was the young German who strode to success, appropriately with fellow European Ballesteros as his playing partner. On that particular day, Langer happened to be wearing a red shirt and red slacks which would hardly be the ideal choice of apparel to tone in with a green jacket. 'I looked like a Christmas tree,' he recalled, after taking considerable care not to make the same mistake on the occasion of his second Masters' triumph in 1993.

The splendid links greens of Portmarnock, though quick, held none of the forbidding qualities of Augusta, as Langer set off in defence of the Irish Open title in 1988. Much was expected of the champion, particularly in view of an astonishing winning aggregate of 267 – 21 under par – the previous year. But the German knew that a repeat performance was no more than a wild dream: the yips had returned, with a vengeance.

'It was pitiful to look at him,' said playing partner Eamonn Darcy, after the champion had missed the cut. But Darcy added prophetically: 'If anyone can beat them, Bernhard can.'

For this, his latest battle with an affliction that had destroyed countless careers, Langer eventually settled on a method that had once been employed by Ian Marchbank, father of current European Tour professional Brian Marchbank. With the right hand gripping the club to his left forearm, Langer gradually regained his confidence on the greens. Eventually, the rehabilitation had been so convincing that when he challenged for another Masters' crown in 1993, the possibility of yet another putting breakdown, was never even considered by the cognoscenti.

Langer, incidentally, had only one three-putt in 72 holes on greens that had been cut to one eighth of an inch for the duration of the tournament. As Henry Cotton had observed, the winners manage.

SHARP'S

THE US OPEN

THE US OPEN

ROLL · OF · HONOUR

1895	Horace Rawlins
1896	James Foulis
1897	Joe Lloyd
1898	Fred Herd
1899	Willie Smith
1900	Harry Vardon
1901	* Willie Anderson
1902	Laurie Auchterlonie
1903	* Willie Anderson
1904	Willie Anderson
1905	Willie Anderson
1906	Alex Smith
1907	Alex Ross
1908	* Fred McLeod
1909	George Sargent
1910	* Alex Smith
1911	* John McDermott
1912	John McDermott
1913	* Francis Ouimet
1914	Walter Hagen
1915	Jerome Travers
1916	Charles Evans, Jr
1917-18	No championships played
1919	* Walter Hagen
1920	Edward Ray
1921	James M. Barnes
1922	Gene Sarazen
1923	* Robert T. Jones
1924	Cyril Walker
1925	* W. MacFarlane
1926	Robert T. Jones
1927	* Tommy Armour
1928	* Johnny Farrell
1929	Robert T. Jones
1930	Robert T. Jones
1931	* Billy Burke
1932	Gene Sarazen
1933	Johnny Goodman
1934	Olin Dutra
1935	Sam Parks, Jr
1936	Tony Manero
1937	Ralph Guldahl
1938	Ralph Guldahl
1939	* Byron Nelson
1940	* Lawson Little
1941	Craig Wood
1942-5	No championships played
1946	* Lloyd Mangrum
1947	* Lew Worsham
1948	Ben Hogan
1949	Cary Middlecoff
1950	* Ben Hogan
1951	Ben Hogan
1952	Julius Boros
1953	Ben Hogan
1954	Ed Furgol
1955	* Jack Fleck
1956	Cary Middlecoff
1957	* Dick Mayer
1958	Tommy Bolt
1959	Billy Casper
1960	Arnold Palmer
1961	Gene Littler
1962	* Jack Nicklaus
1963	* Julius Boros
1964	Ken Venturi
1965	* Gary Player
1966	* Billy Casper
1967	Jack Nicklaus
1968	Lee Trevino
1969	Orville Moody
1970	Tony Jacklin
1971	* Lee Trevino
1972	Jack Nicklaus
1973	Johnny Miller
1974	Hale Irwin
1975	* Lou Graham
1976	Jerry Pate
1977	Hubert Green
1978	Andy North
1979	Hale Irwin
1980	Jack Nicklaus
1981	David Graham
1982	Tom Watson
1983	Larry Nelson
1984	* Fuzzy Zoeller
1985	Andy North
1986	Ray Floyd
1987	Scott Simpson
1988	* Curtis Strange
1989	Curtis Strange
1990	* Hale Irwin
1991	* Payne Stewart
1992	Tom Kite
1993	Lee Janzen

* Winner in play-off.

· HIGHLIGHTS ·

Most wins:
4 Willie Anderson
Bobby Jones
Ben Hogan
Jack Nicklaus

Most times runner-up:
4 Bobby Jones
Sam Snead
Arnold Palmer
Jack Nicklaus

Biggest margin of victory:
9 Willie Smith (1899)
Jim Barnes (1921)

Lowest winning total:
272 Jack Nicklaus (1980)
Lee Janzen (1993)

Lowest single round:
63 Johnny Miller (1973)
Tom Weiskopf (1980)
Jack Nicklaus (1980)

Lowest final round by winner:
63 Johnny Miller (1973)

Oldest champion:
Hale Irwin, aged 45 (1990)

Youngest champion:
Johnny McDermott, aged 19 (1911)

THE 1993 US OPEN

The Masters may have more glamour and the British Open more history but for American golfers the US Open is the ultimate prize

In June 1993 Baltusrol, New Jersey hosted the championship for a record seventh time; on the two occasions prior to then, in 1967 and 1980, Jack Nicklaus won his second and fourth titles, establishing record four round totals in the process. Much was therefore expected of the 93rd US Open and, one must assume, much is now expected of the champion it produced.

Great expectations can be heavy burdens. For four hot and humid days last summer unpredictability reigned. Stealing the show at Baltusrol on Day One were two amateur golfers: 16 year-old Ted Oh, the youngest player to qualify for a US Open in 50 years and 21 year-old Justin Leonard who achieved a 69 on Thursday, outscoring his two illustrious playing partners, the defending

Paul Azinger, Nick Price and Bernhard Langer at Baltusrol

A strong finish lifted Ernie Els into the top ten

champion Tom Kite and the British Open champion Nick Faldo. Only 10 players bettered Leonard's 69. Scott Hoch, Joey Sindelar and Craig Parry shared the first round lead with scores of 66, four under par, and a stroke behind them on 67 were Lee Janzen and the mercurial Craig Stadler. It was hardly a heavyweight leaderboard (Craig Stadler excepted).

By Friday evening only Lee Janzen of the early pacemakers was still in the frame but Tom Kite (75-70), Greg Norman (73-74), Seve Ballesteros (76-72) and Bernhard Langer (74-71) were on their way home. The dreaded half-way axe fell at 144, this score being 10 strokes adrift of Janzen whose second

Janzen's 134 total equalled the championship best for 36 holes – the mark having been set, like the four round record score of 272, by Nicklaus in 1980. Still, there was a long way to go and notwithstanding the bluntness of the European challenge, several big names now appeared to have Janzen firmly in their sites as the weekend approached. Payne Stewart and Tom Watson both scored 66s on Friday and they, of course, as the

'Cheesed off' Ian Woosnam couldn't stand the heat

successive 67 included four birdies in a row from the 10th. It was just as well that the 28 year-old from Florida ran out of birdies by the time he reached Baltusrol's 17th tee: both the 17th and 18th are par fives and a four at either one would have caused Britain's Faldo, Woosnam and Lyle to join Ballesteros and Langer on the plane back to Europe.

saying goes, 'had been there before'. Watson and Stewart moved to within two of Janzen while Nick Price and Corey Pavin were also waiting in the wings just a stroke further back. Going into the weekend then we had Janzen on 134; Watson and Stewart on 136 and Price and Pavin on 137.

The heart said Watson but the head said Stewart, Pavin or Price. Janzen was just a pacemaker, wasn't he? The world was about to discover otherwise.

In what was still a fledgling career, Lee Janzen already had two PGA Tour victories to his credit. In 1992 he won the Northern Telecom Open and five months before Baltusrol he captured the Phoenix Open title. His major championship record was less impressive however and in three US Open appearances he had missed the cut on each occasion.

The swing remained as good as ever, but poor putting put paid to Tom Watson's challenge

Paired with Tom Watson in the third round, Janzen wasted no time is dispelling the pacemaker theory. Birdies at the first two holes were followed by a demonstration in the art of consolidation. This was hardly the type of day, mind you, for dashing heroics. To spend the day at Baltusrol on Saturday was akin to spending the day in a Turkish bath. In such oppressive conditions, and on a course measuring well over 7,000 yards, nobody was likely to 'shoot the lights out' and come charging through the field. The only thing cool on Sunday were the putters of Watson and Price. From tee to green the Zimbabwean struck the ball (as he did throughout the year) in a fashion reminiscent of Watson in the late 70s: a brisk, compact swing producing arrow-straight shots that peppered the flagsticks. Watson too was playing more like Tom Watson of old, but sadly both were putting like the Tom Watson of post 1984. Craig Parry and Paul Azinger would eventually finish joint third in the championship and South Africa's Ernie Els scored 68-67 in his last two rounds for an impressive top 10 finish, but by the back nine of the third round the 1993 US Open began to develop into an intriguing head to head contest between Lee Janzen and Payne Stewart. Come the end of steamy Saturday Stewart (68) had narrowed the gap on Janzen (69) to just one. They were seven under and six under par respectively. Price was four behind Janzen but Watson, who drove into water at the 18th, had slipped back to just one under par.

'The ultimate prize for American golfers', we began, 'is the US Open'. Funny then, that Lee Janzen should be standing on the first tee on Sunday dressed more like a baseball player with Payne Stewart beside him garbed in one of his customary American football outfits. Two all-American boys at least.

As on Saturday, nobody in the chasing pack could make much of an impression on the two leaders. Sandy Lyle holed-in-one at the 12th and almost repeated the trick at the 16th but he, like all the Europeans, was never remotely in contention. Janzen started his final round better than Stewart but by the 12th the 1991 champion had caught his younger opponent. Over the closing holes most observers expected that a combination of Stewart's experience and greater length off the tee would bring him his third major triumph. They were wrong, of course. Instead, it was Janzen's short game, allied, it must be said, to a healthy dollop of good fortune that ultimately decided matters.

Payne and frustration: no third Major for Stewart (left). High noon becomes high-fives as Janzen (below) seals it by chipping-in at the 16th

Janzen regained the lead with a 20 foot birdie putt at the 14th. At the short 16th his

Lee Janzen savours the greatest moment of his life

tee shot flirted with the bunkers in front of the green and finished in the rough; Stewart, who was safely on the green, then watched in disbelief as his 'opponent' pitched into the hole for a two – just like Watson at Pebble Beach in 1982. To his credit, Stewart never gave up but when Janzen's drive at the 17th ricocheted off a tree back onto the fairway he knew that this was not destined to be his day. There was still time for a few missed heart beats on the final hole when Janzen's approach to the green skipped past the edge of a deep trap, but it came to rest no more than eight feet from the flag.

Given what he was about to achieve it didn't really matter, but Janzen now realised that he had a putt for a 69 – his fourth score under 70, something only Lee Trevino had managed before in a US Open – and an aggregate total of 272, equalling the championship record. Well, the gods had been with him all day and they were hardly going to desert him now.

The 'ultimate prize' belonged to Lee Janzen. At the start of the final round we had hoped for a dramatic 'Duel in the Sun' encounter. It never approached such epic proportions, but it had its moments and the hero of the hour, a worthy and unexpected champion, did win with a score that matched the very best of Nicklaus and with a decisive stroke that evoked the style of Watson.

1993 US Open

FINAL · SCORES

L Janzen	67	67	69	69	272	$290,000
P Stewart	70	66	68	70	274	145,000
C Parry	66	74	69	68	277	78,556
P Azinger	71	68	69	69	277	78,556
S Hoch	66	72	72	68	278	48,730
T Watson	70	66	73	69	278	48,730
E Els	71	73	68	67	279	35,481
R Floyd	68	73	70	68	279	35,481
N Henke	72	71	67	69	279	35,481
F Funk	70	72	67	70	279	35,481
L Roberts	70	70	71	69	280	26,249
J Sluman	71	71	69	69	280	26,249
J Adams	70	70	69	71	280	26,249
D Edwards	70	72	66	72	280	26,249
N Price	71	66	70	73	280	26,249
B Lane	74	68	70	69	281	21,576
F Couples	68	71	71	71	281	21,576
M Standly	70	69	70	72	281	21,576
B McCallister	68	73	73	68	282	18,071
D Forsman	73	71	70	68	282	18,071
C Pavin	68	69	75	70	282	18,071
T Lehman	71	70	71	70	282	18,071
S Pate	70	71	71	70	282	18,071
I Baker-Finch	70	70	70	72	282	18,071
C Strange	73	68	75	67	283	14,531
N Ozaki	70	70	74	69	283	14,531
R Mediate	68	72	73	70	283	14,531
C Beck	72	68	72	71	283	14,531
K Perry	74	70	68	71	283	14,531
M Calcavecchia	70	70	71	72	283	14,531
J Cook	75	66	70	72	283	14,531
W Levi	71	69	69	74	283	14,531
S Lowery	72	71	75	66	284	11,051
C Montgomerie	71	72	73	68	284	11,051
B Gilder	70	69	75	70	284	11,051
M Ozaki	71	71	72	70	284	11,051
G Twiggs	72	72	70	70	284	11,051
B Andrade	72	67	74	71	284	11,051
L Rinker	70	72	71	71	284	11,051

Following in the footsteps of Nicklaus: Lee Janzen with the US Open trophy

J Daly	72	68	72	72	284	11,051
C Stadler	67	74	71	72	284	11,051
R Allenby	74	69	69	72	284	11,051
D Love III	70	74	68	72	284	11,051
S Elkington	71	70	69	74	284	11,051
M Donald	71	72	67	74	284	11,051
S Simpson	70	73	72	70	285	8,179
M Brooks	72	68	74	71	285	8,179
M McCumber	70	71	73	71	285	8,179
B Claar	71	70	72	72	285	8,179
R Fehr	71	72	70	72	285	8,179
L Nelson	70	71	71	73	285	8,179
K Triplett	70	72	75	69	286	6,525
I Woosnam	70	74	72	70	286	6,525
F Allem	71	70	74	71	286	6,525
V Heafner	70	72	73	71	286	6,525
E Kirby	72	71	72	71	286	6,525
M Christie	70	74	71	71	286	6,525
K Clearwater	71	72	71	72	286	6,525
S Lyle	70	74	70	72	286	6,525
B Estes	71	73	69	73	286	6,525
J Maggert	69	70	73	74	286	6,525
M Hulbert	71	73	72	71	287	5,940
H Irwin	73	71	71	72	287	5,940
M Smith	68	72	74	73	287	5,940
A Knoll	71	70	73	73	287	5,940
J Edwards	71	73	70	73	287	5,940
J D Blake	72	70	71	74	287	5,940

Usual Runners-up, Unusual Winner

A Commentary by Derek Lawrenson

Why do British golfers never win the US Open? I'll tell you why. They are not humble enough. They treat the event as if it's just another tournament. They're still over here when they should be over there and they wonder why they're overwhelmed and bemused come the end of the second round when if they've not missed the cut, they're near to propping up what's left of the field.

This shouldn't be happening to Ian Woosnam, or Colin Montgomerie or Sandy Lyle. Not with their talents. Not with their touch. And certainly not at Baltusrol, where the rough was pared down for the 1993 US Open, and the fairways widened to take account of the daunting length that the Lower Course there possesses.

All three liked their chances on the eve of the tournament. All were complaining after round two. Where's my touch gone? Where's my sense of feel? Well, now, let us see if we can work it out. The previous week all three had been playing in Hamburg where the greens were so slow that some players almost felt like using a long iron to putt with rather than the more traditional club.

All three left for America on the Monday after the event and therefore started practising for the US Open on the Tuesday. Their final practice round came on Wednesday. Now, Sherlock, is 48 hours enough time to get used to greens that possessed the proverbial grease lightening after what the players had experienced in Germany? And if it is, how come Nick Faldo, the best player in the world, felt he needed to be at Baltusrol a full week before in order to give the event his best shot?

Faldo, of course, needs to be exempt from all comment expressed in the opening paragraph. When it comes to the majors no-one's more humble. Faldo thinks there are four tournaments out of the 25 he plays in every year that are special and accordingly he puts in the necessary rehearsal time. Asked about his practice routine for the majors, Faldo said: 'If it does not work this year, I might have to come over a month early next year and set up camp on the first tee.'

Even Severiano Ballesteros, bless him, came over and played in the tournament before the US Open in an effort to reacquaint himself with American tournament conditions. Pity he was hitting the ball sideways all year. For José-Maria Olazabal, ditto.

As it turned out, Faldo was to endure his most disappointing US Open since his first. And with Bernhard Langer, the Masters champion, and the only other European player who takes the tournament seriously enough to be considered a contender, troubled from the off by a neck injury, the US Open remained comfortably out of overseas hands for another year. Barry Lane, playing in his first US Open, was the top European finishing in joint 16th place; no disrespect to Lane, but when you're relying on a rookie to fly the flag, you've got problems.

The event itself had problems too. The US Open was back at Baltusrol for the first time in 13 years. You know, back to just outside Manhattan, where the fans are brash and have a good time and usually revel in spectacular finishes. Like when 'ugly big' Jack Nicklaus defeated Arnold Palmer to win the 1967 Open. Or when 'loveable cuddly' Jack Nicklaus rose from the ashes of a supposedly burnt-out career to win again in 1980.

This was going to be the US Open that erased the memories of all those crashing bores of recent seasons, when the rough was so thick it took the skills away from the shotmakers. Everyone walked into the 'meeja' centre and voiced just this opinion. There were no dissenters. Great course. Great condition. Great tournament.

Two out of three ain't bad, so the song says, and it was, indeed is, a great course and it was in great condition. Unfortunately, the one factor missing was the most important. The event itself was totally forgettable. Indeed six months after it had finished, I attended a sports quiz night where one of the questions asked you to name the 1993 US Open winner and there were puzzled looks everywhere. Actually, Lee Janzen's a rather better player than that cruel assessment suggests.

His was a conventional major championship success since first he learned how to win a routine tournament, then he led a couple of the big four events, and then he learned how to win one. What made it impressive was the speed with which he learned. He had only played in six previous majors. Who would have thought he would travel the final mile so quickly?

Furthermore, he did it in the face of opposition from Payne Stewart, twice a major winner. In hindsight, Stewart might care to reflect that the choice of the Buffalo Bills' colours as his final day uniform was a bad mistake. For a start, if there is one sports team that New Yorkers can't stand it is the one from upstate, the dreaded Buffalo. For another, the Bills are the team that always finishes second. Hasn't Stewart ever heard of a four-letter word called fate?

Dressed in a peaked cap, and an old-fashioned striped shirt, Janzen looked as if he was ready to play baseball. His concentration on that final day was reminiscent of a steely-eyed pitcher. And the last 1500 yards of his journey were laden with good fortune too.

The trouble was it was all, well, just dull. Even the New Yorkers couldn't raise a whoop or a holler. Which was all a shame for Janzen who displayed a major champion's qualities, including at the close that one so elusive to certain Brits, humility. 'To perform at my ultimate best in the most important week will, I'm sure, prove the over-achievement of my life,' he said.

But it won't be the cheers that greeted Janzen's chip-in at the 70th hole that will stay in my memory. Rather, an incident that occurred in the second round that really did get the locals cheering.

The 17th at Baltusrol is 630 yards, uphill, and unreachable in two. So they said. Even Nicklaus didn't make it in his prime. It was, then, a situation that called for one John Daly. Day two found him playing well and driving it long. As he went on to the tee, a roar of anticipation rang out along every yard of this massive hole.

Daly took out his driver; the killer whale. The ball crashed through the ether and came to rest 327 yards away. As Daly caught up with it, the galleries cheered him to the echo. They knew what was coming next. Only problem was, Daly doesn't carry any fairway woods so how was he going to propel the ball another 303 yards on to the green? Simple. Daly did what Daly does. He took out his one iron and swung as hard as he could. He lost his balance. The ball still flew arrow-straight. It pitched 15 yards short, hopped twice and then went on to the green. Daly high-fived a television commentator. He walked among his kind of people and they responded by calling his name again and again. The 1993 US Open never got any better than this.

The Open Championship

The Open Championship

ROLL · OF · HONOUR

1860	Willie Park
1861	Tom Morris, Sr
1862	Tom Morris, Sr
1863	Willie Park
1864	Tom Morris, Sr
1865	Andrew Strath
1866	Willie Park
1867	Tom Morris, Sr
1868	Tom Morris, Jr
1869	Tom Morris, Jr
1870	Tom Morris, Jr
1871	No championships played
1872	Tom Morris, Jr
1873	Tom Kidd
1874	Mungo Park
1875	Willie Park
1876	Bob Martin
1877	Jamie Anderson
1878	Jamie Anderson
1879	Jamie Anderson
1880	Robert Ferguson
1881	Robert Ferguson
1882	Robert Ferguson
1883	* Willie Fernie
1884	Jack Simpson
1885	Bob Martin
1886	David Brown
1887	Willie Park, Jr
1888	Jack Burns
1889	* Willie Park, Jr
1890	John Ball
1891	Hugh Kirkaldy
1892	Harold H. Hilton
1893	William Auchterlonie
1894	John H. Taylor
1895	John H. Taylor
1896	* Harry Vardon
1897	Harold H. Hilton
1898	Harry Vardon
1899	Harry Vardon
1900	John H. Taylor
1901	James Braid
1902	Alexander Herd
1903	Harry Vardon
1904	Jack White
1905	James Braid
1906	James Braid
1907	Arnaud Massy
1908	James Braid
1909	John H. Taylor
1910	James Braid
1911	Harry Vardon
1912	Edward Ray
1913	John H. Taylor
1914	Harry Vardon
1915-19	No championships played
1920	George Duncan
1921	* Jock Hutchison
1922	Walter Hagen
1923	Arthur G. Havers

1924	Walter Hagen
1925	James M. Barnes
1926	Robert T. Jones
1927	Robert T. Jones
1928	Walter Hagen
1929	Walter Hagen
1930	Robert T. Jones
1931	Tommy D. Armour
1932	Gene Sarazen
1933	* Denny Shute
1934	Henry Cotton
1935	Alfred Perry
1936	Alfred Padgham
1937	Henry Cotton
1938	R. A. Whitcombe
1939	Richard Burton
1940-45	No championships played
1946	Sam Snead
1947	Fred Daly
1948	Henry Cotton
1949	* Bobby Locke
1950	Bobby Locke
1951	Max Faulkner
1952	Bobby Locke
1953	Ben Hogan
1954	Peter Thomson
1955	Peter Thomson
1956	Peter Thomson
1957	Bobby Locke
1958	* Peter Thomson
1959	Gary Player
1960	Kel Nagle
1961	Arnold Palmer
1962	Arnold Palmer
1963	* Bob Charles
1964	Tony Lema
1965	Peter Thomson
1966	Jack Nicklaus
1967	Roberto De Vicenzo
1968	Gary Player
1969	Tony Jacklin
1970	* Jack Nicklaus
1971	Lee Trevino
1972	Lee Trevino
1973	Tom Weiskopf
1974	Gary Player
1975	* Tom Watson
1976	Johnny Miller
1977	Tom Watson
1978	Jack Nicklaus
1979	Seve Ballesteros
1980	Tom Watson
1981	Bill Rogers
1982	Tom Watson
1983	Tom Watson
1984	Seve Ballesteros
1985	Sandy Lyle
1986	Greg Norman
1987	Nick Faldo
1988	Seve Ballesteros
1989	* Mark Calcavecchia
1990	Nick Faldo
1991	Ian Baker-Finch
1992	Nick Faldo
1993	Greg Norman

* Winner in play-off.

· HIGHLIGHTS ·

Most wins:

6 Harry Vardon
5 Hohn H. Taylor
James Braid
Peter Thomson
Tom Watson

Most times runner-up:

7 Jack Nicklaus

Biggest margin of victory:

13 Old Tom Morris (1862)

Lowest winning total:

267 Greg Norman (1993)

Lowest single round:

63 Mark Hayes (1977)
Isao Aoki (1980)
Greg Norman (1986)
Paul Broadhurst (1990)
Jodie Mudd (1991)
Nick Faldo (1993)
Payne Stewart (1993)

Lowest final round by winner:

64 Greg Norman (1993)
65 Tom Watson (1977)
Severiano Ballesteros (1988)

Oldest champion:

Old Tom Morris, aged 46 (1867)

Youngest champion:

Young Tom Morris, aged 17 (1868)
Severiano Ballesteros (youngest this century, aged 22 in 1979)

THE 1993 OPEN CHAMPIONSHIP

St George's, July 18, 1993: the Dragon is dead; long live the Shark

A vast gallery of privileged, excited and amazed spectators lines the 18th fairway at St George's as Bernhard Langer turns to Greg Norman and says, 'that was the best golf I have ever seen. You deserve to win.'

The German golfer must have played, never mind witnessed, many of golf's finest rounds but the 1993 Masters champion meant every word of his generous compliment.

Moments after he had two putted for a 64 and been crowned Open champion for the second time, Norman added a few of his own sentiments and reflected that he had never before played 18 holes during which he 'hit every drive perfect and every iron shot perfect.'

Although disciples of the player pictured opposite may beg to differ, Greg Norman is probably the only golfer on Earth who could have out-charged a charging Arnold Palmer. Remember in this same championship the incredible 63 at windswept Turnberry in 1986, or the 64 at Troon three years later when he began his final round with six straight birdies? He has had 62s at such revered courses as Doral's Blue Monster and Canada's Glen Abbey, and there have been 63s in such contrasting places as St Andrews and Tryall in Jamaica. But this, he reckoned, topped the lot. Given the quality of the leaderboard on Saturday night the 1993 Open was always going to be a great championship to win. Marvellous it was then, that it should

'Reports of my demise have been greatly exaggerated': Greg Norman silenced his critics with a brilliant 64

have been won in such glorious fashion.

Yet, how horribly it all began for the winner! At his very first hole on Thursday Greg 'hacked' his way to a double bogey six; this on a course whose natural fury had been severely dampened by a heavy downpour on Tuesday evening. Prior to the rain, St George's had threatened to humiliate this gathering of the world's elite. During Monday's practice round tee shots, 'ricocheted around fairways like a ping-pong match in a fiery oven', Gary Van Sickle graphically wrote in Australian Golf Digest. Come the first round of the 123rd Open, however, good drives tended to finish close to where they had landed – even if that meant the occasional awkward stance on a rippling, tumbling fairway.

Thursday was the kind of day where if you didn't beat the par of 70 you lost ground. Four players scored 66s and many more returned 67s and 68s. The defending champion, Nick Faldo, could 'only' manage a 69 but several of the anticipated challengers took advantage of the relatively favourable conditions. Nick Price, Fred Couples, Corey Pavin, Ernie Els and Seve Ballesteros were among those who took 68. Seve's score included a disappointing five-five finish but he was nonetheless pleased with a round that belied his recent poor form. (In 1985, the last time the Open had been staged on the Kent coast, the Spaniard was the defending champion and pre-tournament favourite and Sandy Lyle emerged as the eventual winner – how times change!) Langer was in the group who shot 67 and, amazingly, given that horrid opening hole, Norman joined Fuzzy Zoeller, Mark Calcavecchia and fellow Australian Peter Senior at the head of the field with a 66.

Eight birdies (and two bogeys) followed Norman's six at the 1st and on the back nine he birdied five holes in succession from the 13th – so much for the course's formidable finishing stretch. But St George's reputation as a stern examination was destined for an even greater battering on Day Two.

If there is one thing that regularly seems to inspire Nick Faldo it is a burst of sub-par golf from Greg Norman. Remember St Andrews in 1990 and the aforementioned 'duel in Jamaica'? Palmer's legendary charges used to have a similar effect on Jack Nicklaus and although it is perhaps as premature as it is

Seve's style of play thrilled (and occasionally threatened) the galleries at St George's

flattering to compare the Englishman's game with that of the Golden Bear at his peak, he does seem to possess a comparable ability to raise his game when the occasion merits. Friday was emphatically Faldo's day at the Open, just as it had been 12 months earlier at Muirfield when his 64 established a 36 hole championship record of 130. This time he went one better with a course record 63. It was simply brilliant and, with seven birdies and 11 pars, blemish free. The highlight was undoubtedly the drive – two-iron – 15 foot putt birdie he made at the 18th. So, 69 plus 63 equals 132: the defending champion had laid down the gauntlet.

To be fair to the supporting cast (because that's all they really were in the second round) while none picked up the proverbial glove and ran off with it, some did at least attempt to juggle with it. John Daly, for instance: after a modest one over par 71 in the first round he got himself to five under for the championship after 16 holes but unfortunately took six at the 17th. (Daly, incidentally, managed to drive the green at the 421-yards 5th hole during practice). English amateur golfer, Iain Pyman also soared to five under par at one stage and into a share of third place before inevitably stumbling on the back nine. Pyman went on to finish a very creditable joint 28th and set a new record amateur total for the championship of 281. Couples, rather like Daly, had a 'what might have been' round as he bogeyed the last two holes for a 66 to end two behind Faldo, and Langer also bogeyed the 18th for a 66 to be just one stroke adrift of Faldo on 133. Norman, with a 68, and Pavin (66), joined Couples at six under par to create an extremely impressive leaderboard.

For two days Ian Woosnam had the pleasure of John Daly's company (left). Nick Faldo (above) during his round of 63 on Friday

What of Seve on Friday? Sadly, like his compatriot, Olazabal he retreated to the wilderness – quite literally at times; indeed Seve seemed to spend more time in the rough than on the fairway. There was, however, still one flash of Spanish genius when from deep in the hay to the left of the 15th he pitched into the hole with a nine-iron from 112 yards. Like the Armada, he was determined to go down with all guns blazing.

Fred Couples missed the occasional fairway, but was in contention for much of the week

Poor Seve. And poor old St George – beaten to its knees by a barrage of birdies. But the course fought back on Saturday and, if the ultimate test of a championship course is its ability to sift the great from the good, then it passed with flying colours on Sunday.

Saturday turned out to be tread-water day. The wind blew a little stronger and the flags appeared in a few peculiar and unwelcome places. As a result, Old Man Par was welcomed back like a long lost friend. Faldo made 16 in his round of 70 and maintained his overnight lead (albeit now shared). His playing partner Langer also scored a 70 and for once even Greg Norman bore the air of a man intent on consolidating his position as he reeled off 15 pars in a very workmanlike 69. As for the Americans, Couples slipped back a little with a 72 but Pavin moved forwards with a 68. It was chess without any checkmates: hardly scintillating stuff, but very strategic. The two players who threatened to make significant progress on Saturday were Nick Price and Ernie Els. Both went to the turn in 32 (Els scoring six threes in his first eight holes) but they came home in 35 and 37 respectively.

The leaderboard was always going to be Saturday's saving grace. We all knew that minimal changes in the third round only increased the likelihood of a serious shoot-out on Sunday. Three-quarters of the way through the championship, then, Faldo and Pavin led the way with eight under par totals of 202; Norman and Langer were hard on their heels on 203, and three behind on 205 were Price and Senior. Couples, Els and Grady were a further shot back on 206.

Sunday at Sandwich. It was the defending

champion's birthday and patriotism was rife. 'England expects... St Nick to be crowned at St George's... Faldo to collect his fourth title in seven years.' The presumptions were understandable but inaccurate. Friday had been Faldo's day but Sunday belonged to the Shark; Nick played superbly but Greg played sublimely. These two great rivals were the key figures on a day of high drama but several other players also contributed to make the final round of the 1993 Open one of the greatest days in major championship history.

It is not difficult to picture American Payne Stewart holding aloft the famous claret jug. He always looks the part and, when the mood takes him, he has the ability to play it. For three days however he did little of any consequence but on Sunday Stewart went out early and matched Faldo's two-day old course record, his 63 comprising a tidy nine threes and nine fours. Luckily for the leaders he was never in contention. Scotland's Paul Lawrie holed out with a three-iron for an eagle at the 17th in a round of 65 and South African Ernie Els, a future winner of majors if ever there was one, chipped-in for a birdie at the 1st, but for any of this to matter the final pairings needed to start slowly and of course they didn't. Nick Price summed it up when he said, 'even after I birdied two of the first five holes I was trying to hole four-irons to catch up'. Norman and Langer birdied the 1st; Faldo and Pavin birdied the 2nd and Norman birdied the 3rd. When the Australian gained a third birdie

Bernhard Langer watches as another Greg Norman drive is smashed straight down the middle

(Top left) Ernie Els became the first ever player to score four rounds in the 60s; (top right) Nick Faldo settles for second place; (lower left) Payne Stewart equals Faldo's 63 and (lower right) Corey Pavin seeks help from an outside agency

The final moments of a great championship: Langer and Norman leave the 72nd green

at the short 6th, the famous 'Maiden', he took the lead. Pavin couldn't quite live with the pace but Faldo, who also birdied the 6th, almost holed-in-one at the 11th in a bold and desperate attempt to close the gap on the leader. But Norman continued to pile on the pressure. Driving the ball majestically, he struck his approach shots to within six inches of the flag at the 9th and 14th, and to within four feet at the 12th and 16th; on each occasion he made a birdie. Incredibly, Langer matched his partner's tally of seven birdies but one uncharacteristic mistake – a drive hit out of bounds at the 14th – cost him a seven, and although he surrounded this double bogey with four birdies the error was critical. The Australian's two at the 16th (his third of the round) proved the decisive birdie as Faldo was unable to repeat the 'four best holes of my life' type finish that had swept him to victory at Muirfield. Norman did miss a very short putt at the 17th but an arrow-straight drive at the last, followed by a rifled four-iron to the heart of the green secured him the title.

No wonder the vast gallery was excited and amazed. Norman's 64 was the lowest ever final round by a champion and his total of 267 broke Tom Watson's 16 year-old championship record. Special guest at the prize giving ceremony was the 1932 Open champion, Gene Sarazen. 'Are they football scores or golf scores?', asked the 91 year-old, who was as excited and amazed as everyone else. Then, endorsing Langer's comments, he declared 'that was the most awesome display and the greatest championship I have seen in my 70 years in golf.'

Greater, even, than the 1935 Masters?

1993 Open Championship

FINAL · SCORES

G Norman	**66**	**68**	**69**	**64**	**267**	**£100,000**
N Faldo	69	63	70	67	269	80,000
B Langer	67	66	70	67	270	67,000
C Pavin	68	66	68	70	272	50,500
P Senior	66	69	70	67	272	50,500
N Price	68	70	67	69	274	33,166
E Els	68	69	69	68	274	33,166
P Lawrie	72	68	69	65	274	33,166
W Grady	74	68	64	69	275	25,500
F Couples	68	66	72	69	275	25,500
S Simpson	68	70	71	66	275	25,500
P Stewart	71	72	70	63	276	21,500
B Lane	70	68	71	68	277	20,500
J Daly	71	66	70	71	278	15,214
F Zoeller	66	70	71	71	278	15,214
G Morgan	70	68	70	70	278	15,214
J Rivero	68	73	67	70	278	15,214
M McNulty	67	71	71	69	278	15,214
M Calcavecchia	66	73	71	68	278	15,214
T Kite	72	70	68	68	278	15,214
H Clark	67	72	70	70	279	10,000
J Parnevik	68	74	68	69	279	10,000
P Baker	70	67	74	68	279	10,000
R Davis	68	71	71	70	280	8,400
D Frost	69	73	70	68	280	8,400
M Roe	70	71	73	66	280	8,400
L Mize	67	69	74	71	281	7,225
S Ballesteros	68	73	69	71	281	7,225
M James	70	70	70	71	281	7,225
D Smyth	67	74	70	70	281	7,225
Y Mizumaki	69	69	73	70	281	7,225
M Mackenzie	72	71	71	67	281	7,225
I Pyman	68	72	70	71	281	Am.
H Twitty	71	71	67	73	282	6,180
R Floyd	70	72	67	73	282	6,180
W Westner	67	73	72	70	282	6,180

Congratulations from 91 year-old Gene Sarazen

P Broadhurst	71	69	74	68	282	6,180
J Van de Velde	75	67	73	67	282	6,180
D Clarke	69	71	69	74	283	5,327
C O'Connor Jnr	72	68	69	74	283	5,327
A Sorensen	69	70	72	72	283	5,327
D Waldorf	68	71	73	71	283	5,327
P Moloney	70	71	71	71	283	5,327
G Turner	67	76	70	70	283	5,327
C Mason	69	73	72	69	283	5,327
A Magee	71	72	71	69	283	5,327
R Mediate	71	71	72	69	283	5,327
L Janzen	69	71	73	71	284	4,850
S Elkington	72	71	71	70	284	4,850
J Huston	68	73	76	67	284	4,850
J Sewell	70	72	69	74	285	4,356
M Pinero	70	72	71	72	285	4,356
F Nobilo	69	70	74	72	285	4,356
S Torrance	72	70	72	71	285	4,356
M A Jimenez	69	74	72	70	285	4,356
I Woosnam	72	71	72	70	285	4,356
S Ames	67	75	73	70	285	4,356
I Garbutt	68	75	73	69	285	4,356
C Parry	72	69	71	74	286	4,025
T Lehman	69	71	73	73	286	4,025
V Singh	69	72	72	73	286	4,025
P Azinger	69	73	74	70	286	4,025

Fighting Back

A Commentary by Lauren St John

The decline and rise of Greg Norman is a story best illustrated by those moments in his career which live on most vividly in our memories. Unforgettable are the images of Norman etched against a stormy sky at Turnberry in 1986, his face contorted with determination as he lashed furiously from the rough en route to his first major title; waving a white towel in surrender to Fuzzy Zoeller after the 1984 US Open play-off and, finally, smiling through tear-rimmed blue eyes at St George's in July, as he ended seven years of torment and doubt with one of the greatest final rounds in Open history.

'That, to me, is the test of the true character of an individual,' Norman said. 'How you win and how you lose.'

Professional golf is nothing if not a gamble, a lifelong flirtation with the elements, the psyche and the intangibles of the golf swing. Until the white towel of surrender became a symbol of Norman's inadequacies, every hand destiny dealt him held an ace. A shy teenager with dreams of becoming a fighter pilot, he became a flamboyant and gregarious golfer with Palmeresque glamour, who lived fast and played harder, gathering Ferraris and million-dollar endorsements at much the same rate as he picked up victories.

But, inevitably, there came a day when Norman's luck ran out, when the gun in the roulette game he was playing failed to register a reassuring click and exploded in his face instead. That occasion was at Augusta in 1986, when Norman carved his aproach shot into the gallery and took five. Numerous others followed. Norman saw Bob Tway sink a fluke bunker shot in the 1986 USPGA Championship, watched aghast as Larry Mize holed an impossible 40-yard chip shot to steal the 1987 Masters title, and bunkered his drive at Troon's 18th hole to lose a play-off for the 1989 Open Championship.

Any one of these blows would have finished a lesser player. Norman, however, turned every negative into a positive, as though crushing defeats were essential pieces in the jigsaw of great golf. 'The whole crux of the deal is that you believe in yourself and don't believe fate's against you and don't believe in bad luck,' he said. 'You have to love the game with enough heart to say, 'I can bounce back from whatever they throw at me. Whether it's next year or the year after, I know somewhere down the line I'll be able to do it, and things will turn around and maybe I'll be the one to hole my second shot.'

Nevertheless, the constant drip, drip, dripping of failure, media interrogation and self-denigration had a water-torture effect on Norman. It wore down his defences. He did not merely become a shadow of his former self; he became a ghostly, even ghastly, parody of the champion he had once been. He dieted so much that he seemed shrunken, in spirit as well as in body, and he slunk around the world's best tournaments like some borderline pro fearful of meeting his bank manager. In 20 months he went from being a great golden force of a man to being a lank-haired and unprepossessing (albeit extremely rich) member of the pack. Soon, Norman's nickname became a handle on which to hang the skeletons of what might have been. The Great White Shark became the Great White Carp or, more cruelly, the Great White Flag.

True, Norman had given notice of his return to form at the end of 1992 by winning the Canadian Open and giving a command performance in the Johnnie Walker World Championship before losing to Nick Faldo. He had also recorded four top-three finishes early in 1993, and had tossed aside Miami's infamous 'Blue Monster' course like an unwanted teddy bear in the Doral Ryder Open, shooting a 10-birdie 62 which later gave him victory by four strokes. But his results in the majors had been dismal. A tie for 31st in the Masters and a missed cut in the US Open lent weight to the argument that at 38, Norman could be written off as a one-major wonder.

Why Norman escaped this fate, and instead staged one of the most spectacular comebacks in sport, is open to debate. Winston Churchill once said that success was going from failure to failure without loss of self-esteem. Like Faldo, Norman has the confidence to analyse his game and realise that his technique, rather than an innate inability to withstand pressure, might be at fault. He sought the help of American coach Butch Harmon. Together, they set about building a flatter, more consistent swing that would eliminate the blocked drive and perilously spinning approach that has cost Norman so dearly.

Norman admits that when they began, he was his own worst enemy, frustrated and down on himself. 'I re-evaluated what I wanted. I could have walked away but I didn't. I wanted to get back to playing good golf. To do that you have to practice hard. And to do that, you have to prioritise.'

Number one on the Australian's agenda was, of course, winning major titles. To help him do this, he enlisted the aid of a small team of dedicated professionals, namely Harmon, Tony Navaro, an American caddie of 20 years experience, Hughes Norton, his personal manager, Peter, his fitness trainer, who put Norman through 45 minutes of gruelling stretching exercises every morning, and John Cott, his Irish chauffeur.

Norman freely acknowledges the part his entourage have played in his success, but there is little doubt that without an extraordinary amount of drive and discipline, he would never have arrived at the state of grace which at the Open saw him compile one of the most awe-inspiring rounds golf has witnessed. 'I missed being the No.1 player in the world,' Norman replied frankly, when asked what he felt the key to his resurgence was. 'I've had it, I've felt it, I've experienced it before. I know I can handle it. I know what goes with it.

He admitted that there had been a time when that wasn't true. 'Everybody goes through a phase in life – they'd be telling lies if they said they didn't – where they don't want to do something. We all get sick and bored with certain things we do in life. That happened to me in '91 and '92. And if anybody tells me they've never experienced that in their own field, I know they're lying because it's human nature. How much of that you go through depends on how strong you are and how quickly you can pull yourself up.'

At St George's he seemed to have regained his belief that loss of confidence is a superficial deal. 'If your mind is strong on the negative side, you'll never play great golf, but if it's strong on the positive side then you're going to be around for a long time, no matter what people say or do to you.'

With this in mind, Norman has devised a seven year plan which will take him to the turn of the century. His ambitions are the same as they always have been. 'You can set yourself goals and you can go about trying to attain them, but you can also just say to yourself: I want to be the best I can be, I don't want to settle for anything else. If you settle for second best, then you're a loser.'

The USPGA

The USPGA

ROLL · OF · HONOUR

Five-time USPGA champion, Jack Nicklaus shares the record number of wins with Walter Hagen

1916	James M. Barnes
1917-18	No championships played
1919	James M. Barnes
1920	Jock Hutchison
1921	Walter Hagen
1922	Gene Sarazen
1923	Gene Sarazen
1924	Walter Hagen
1925	Walter Hagen
1926	Walter Hagen
1927	Walter Hagen
1928	Leo Diegel
1929	Leo Diegel
1930	Tommy Armour
1931	Tom Creavy
1932	Olin Dutra
1933	Gene Sarazen
1934	Paul Runyan
1935	Johnny Revolta
1936	Denny Shute
1937	Denny Shute
1938	Paul Runyan
1939	Henry Picard
1940	Byron Nelson
1941	Vic Ghezzi
1942	Sam Snead
1943	No championship played
1944	Bob Hamilton
1945	Byron Nelson
1946	Ben Hogan
1947	Jim Ferrier
1948	Ben Hogan
1949	Sam Snead
1950	Chandler Harper
1951	Sam Snead
1952	Jim Turnesa
1953	Walter Burkemo
1954	Chick Harbert
1955	Doug Ford
1956	Jack Burke
1957	Lionel Hebert
1958	Dow Finsterwald
1959	Bob Rosburg
1960	Jay Hebert
1961	* Jerry Barber
1962	Gary Player
1963	Jack Nicklaus
1964	Bobby Nichols
1965	Dave Marr
1966	Al Geiberger
1967	* Don January
1968	Julius Boros
1969	Ray Floyd
1970	Dave Stockton
1971	Jack Nicklaus
1972	Gary Player
1973	Jack Nicklaus
1974	Lee Trevino
1975	Jack Nicklaus
1976	Dave Stockton
1977	* Lanny Wadkins
1978	* John Mahaffey
1979	* David Graham
1980	Jack Nicklaus
1981	Larry Nelson
1982	Ray Floyd
1983	Hal Sutton
1984	Lee Trevino
1985	Hubert Green
1986	Bob Tway
1987	* Larry Nelson
1988	Jeff Sluman
1989	Payne Stewart
1990	Wayne Grady
1991	John Daly
1992	Nick Price
1993	* Paul Azinger

* Winner in play-off.

· HIGHLIGHTS ·

Most wins:
5 Walter Hagen
Jack Nicklaus

Most times runner-up:
4 Jack Nicklaus

Biggest margin of victory:
7 Jack Nicklaus (1980)

Lowest winning total:
271 Bobby Nichols (1964)

Lowest single round:
63 Bruce Crampton (1975)
Ray Floyd (1982)
Gary Player (1984)
Vijay Singh (1993)

Lowest final round by winner:
65 David Graham (1979)
Jeff Sluman (1988)

Oldest champion:
Julius Boros, aged 48 (1968)

Youngest champion:
Gene Sarazen, aged 20 (1922)

THE 1993 USPGA

Inverness, Ohio: it may not be the greatest course ever to have hosted the final major of the year, but, of the 74 'PGAs that preceded 1993's event it is possible that none exceeded the quality of this one

The USPGA Championship is often denigrated – 'the Cinderella of the Majors', it is sometimes called – but here was a genuine classic and, coming so soon after the thrilling final day's play at Sandwich, it was almost as surprising as it was enthralling.

Of course the 'PGA had visited Inverness before; Bob Tway famously holing his bunker shot at the 72nd hole in 1986 to deny Greg Norman a second successive major victory. As well as excitement then, there was an element of déjà vu about the 1993 championship. Bob Tway certainly wasn't the reason, for while he hadn't disappeared altogether he had nonetheless vanished from the face of our television sets. But Greg Norman was back to play a principal role, and he was back as the Open Champion.

The Australian's stunning final round 64 at Royal St George's was still the talk of golf when the players assembled at Inverness – just as his second round 63 and storming five shot victory at Turnberry had been seven years earlier. Norman was therefore the obvious favourite but Nick Faldo, Nick Price, Paul Azinger and Payne Stewart all appeared to be enjoying a rich vein of form and a keen

Nick Faldo with his faithful caddie at Inverness

contest was anticipated – at least that's how the world at large saw things. A poll taken among American golf writers on the eve of the championship confirmed Norman as the man to beat. Apparently each was asked to select a winner and name his or her second and third choices with points being awarded on a 3-2-1 basis. Fifteen plumped for a Norman victory; 8 apiece went for Stewart and Price and 6 for Azinger. Despite his record in the big events

No wonder he's smiling – Vijay Singh (above) has just scored a 63. Veteran Lanny Wadkins (right) made a bold attempt to win his second USPGA title

not one person picked Faldo to win his sixth major title and, perhaps even more amazingly, when all the points were added up he finished with a lower total then either Chip Beck or Jeff Maggert. No comment (none needed!)

Inverness is regarded as a tough, uncompromising layout and it would hardly have been selected to stage the USPGA Championship if otherwise, but during the week of last year's 'PGA it was in a very benign mood. The greens were soft and relatively slow and for four days there was barely a breath of wind. As a result the best players in the world took the course apart;

there were birdies galore, eagles aplenty and even, for the first time in eight years in a major championship, an albatross.

An unknown club professional named Darrell Kestner achieved what in America is called a double-eagle in Thursday's opening round. Scott Simpson, the 1987 US Open champion, led the field after that first day's play with a 64. Lanny Wadkins scored a 65 and no fewer than a record 57 golfers bettered the par of 71. Norman and Faldo both returned 68s and Azinger had a 69. Stewart (with a modest 71) and Price (a poor 74) never really featured in the proceedings.

By Friday, 'par' was fast becoming a dirty word. Fijian Vijay Singh, who had started with a 68, added a superb course record 63 on the second day for a half-way total of 131, 11 under par. It was a blistering pace and a score which normally would have spread-eagled the field but on this occasion all it gave him was a two shot lead over Wadkins and Steve Elkington, with Tom Watson and Simpson a further shot back.

Watson was especially happy with life. Bidding to become only the fifth player to possess a full set of major championship titles, he declared, 'I haven't played like this in years.' Azinger scored a 66 in the second round and Faldo and Norman again matched each other with 68s to remain very much in contention. Faldo's score could have been a great deal better but for a treble bogey seven at the 15th. Prior to this lapse, according to one of his playing partners, Wadkins, he had been playing, 'so damn well it was scary.' The best comment, however, came from someone in the gallery and was overheard by this book's principal photographer, David Cannon: 'Hey, that Vijay Singh guy... do you think he speaks English?'

Although the leaders were unable to pull away from the field there was certainly no let up in the general standard of play on Saturday. Singh lost his magical touch on the greens in the third round but Wadkins holed out from 143 yards with an eight iron, Tom Watson chipped-in twice and Greg Norman did so once. The Open champion's shot was especially relevant as it helped him score a 67 and lifted him to the top of the leaderboard. Déjà vu once again: Norman had led on his own after three rounds in 1986. There was one significant difference on this occasion, however, in that Norman's lead was just one; seven years earlier he had enjoyed a four stroke lead going into the final round.

It was, in fact, an incredibly crowded leaderboard. Watson, Azinger, Singh, Wadkins, Estes and Irwin all finished their rounds just one behind the Australian at nine under par. Another four players including Nick Faldo were two strokes away. In all, 11 players were within two shots of the lead. It was the stuff that sleepless nights are made of.

The prize was the splendid Wanamaker Trophy, $300,000 and a place in history. Norman was seeking to become the first player since Walter Hagen in 1924 to win the British Open and the USPGA title in the same year. Watson, as mentioned above, was playing for even higher stakes. Wadkins was chasing his second major championship success, Irwin his fourth and Faldo his sixth, whilst Azinger and Singh were trying for their first majors and Estes his first tournament victory.

For much of Sunday it seemed possible that Singh or Estes might pull off a shock victory. The most experienced players, Watson, Wadkins and Irwin all fell away fairly quickly, the former eventually repeating his fifth place finish in the US Open. Faldo and Azinger started steadily rather than spectacularly and Norman set off to play a typical Norman round. Partnering Irwin at the back of the field, the Great White Shark birdied the 3rd to move two ahead but then double bogeyed the short 6th after failing to get out of a bunker at the first attempt and immediately dropped another stroke at the 7th. Ahead of Norman, Estes started to wobble and Singh was about to begin a frustrating back nine but Faldo and then Azinger both stepped up a gear.

Following six straight pars the English player, desperate to turn around a year which by his high standards had been disappointing, birdied the 7th and the 8th and took the lead with a birdie four at the 13th. Azinger responded with a hatrick of birdies from the 12th to join him at 11 under par. When Norman bogeyed the 7th he had slipped back to eight under. Memories of his last day collapse in 1986 were returning. Courageously, Norman quickly fought back with a birdie at the 8th. At the 10th he missed a very short putt for another three but managed to join Azinger and Faldo with birdies at the 11th and 13th. The stage was set for a grand finale.

The closing stretch at Inverness is probably the most difficult sequence of holes on the course. Faldo, playing a few holes in front of Azinger and Norman, parred every one of them and had a good opportunity of extracting a birdie from the 16th but missed from four feet. His 68 gave him a total of 273, 11 under par and he had succeeded in breaking 70 in all four rounds. He must have thought his score good enough to force a tie at least but Norman hit his approach to two feet at the 16th and the amazing Azinger did likewise at the 17th. It meant that both overtook Faldo and both had again bettered 70 in each of their rounds.

Major play-offs are not Greg Norman's forte. In 1984 he lost out to Fuzzy Zoeller in the US Open; in 1987 Larry Mize dramatically 'stole' a Green Jacket from under his nose at

Paul Azinger nurses a putt towards the hole during the third round; (left) still no grandslam for Tom Watson

Hale Irwin (above) watches Greg Norman at the 72nd; (right) Paul Azinger captures his first Major title at the second play-off hole

Augusta and Mark Calcavecchia got the better of him in the 1989 Open Championship at Royal Troon. Now it was the turn of a fourth American, Paul Azinger.

Quite how Norman's 18 foot birdie putt at the first sudden death hole avoided dropping is certain to remain one of golf's greatest mysteries: 'one of the nastiest lip-outs you will ever see', according to the generous Azinger, and the way he three putted to lose at the next was a cruel way for it all to end. 'When I've had a couple of beers I'll be all right' said a stunned Shark. 'I can handle adversity pretty good'. He also said of Azinger, 'I lost to a great player. I wish it was me but I'm happy for him because it's his first Major.' Magnanimous in victory at Sandwich, now gracious in defeat at Inverness. Déjà vu and destiny may not be his greatest friends, but what a credit to the game.

1993 USPGA

FINAL · SCORES

Paul Azinger poses with the giant Wanamaker trophy

P Azinger	**69**	**66**	**69**	**68**	**272**	**$300,000**
G Norman	68	68	67	69	272	155,000
(Azinger won play-off at 2nd extra hole)						
N Faldo	68	68	69	68	273	105,000
V Singh	68	63	73	70	274	90,000
T Watson	69	65	70	72	276	75,000
S Hoch	74	68	68	67	277	47,812
N Henke	72	70	67	68	277	47,812
P Mickelson	67	71	69	70	277	47,812
J Cook	72	66	68	71	277	47,812
S Simpson	64	70	71	72	277	47,812
D Hart	66	68	71	72	277	47,812
B Estes	69	66	69	73	277	47,812
H Irwin	68	69	67	73	277	47,812
B Fleisher	69	74	67	68	278	25,000
R Zokol	66	71	71	70	278	25,000
S Elkington	67	66	74	71	278	25,000
G Hallberg	70	69	68	71	278	25,000
B Faxon	70	70	65	73	278	25,000
L Wadkins	65	68	71	74	278	25,000
E Romero	67	67	74	71	279	18,500
J Haas	69	68	70	72	279	18,500
G Sauers	68	74	70	69	281	14,500
F Nobilo	69	66	74	72	281	14,500
L Janzen	70	68	71	72	281	14,500
I Woosnam	70	71	68	72	281	14,500
G Twiggs	70	69	70	72	281	14,500
J McGovern	71	67	69	74	281	14,500
P Jacobsen	71	67	76	72	282	10,166
B Mayfair	68	73	70	71	282	10,166
L Roberts	67	67	77	68	282	10,166
M Calcavecchia	68	70	77	68	283	7,057
M McCumber	67	72	75	69	283	7,057
D Love III	70	72	72	69	283	7,057
S Ingraham	74	69	71	69	283	7,057
F Zoeller	72	70	71	70	283	7,057
N Price	74	66	72	71	283	7,057
T Wargo	71	70	71	71	283	7,057
F Allem	70	71	70	72	283	7,057
M Hulbert	67	72	72	72	283	7,057
H Sutton	69	72	70	72	283	7,057
C Parry	70	73	68	72	283	7,057
F Couples	70	68	71	74	283	7,057
W Levi	69	73	66	75	283	7,057
F Funk	72	66	76	70	284	4,607
D A Weibring	68	74	72	70	284	4,607
R Cochran	69	74	70	71	284	4,607
J Huston	68	69	75	72	284	4,607
D Forsman	67	75	70	72	284	4,607
P Stewart	71	70	70	73	284	4,607
N Ozaki	73	68	66	77	284	4,607
A Magee	71	72	74	68	285	3,600
J Daly	71	68	73	73	285	3,600
J Maggert	72	69	71	73	285	3,600
H Green	70	71	69	75	285	3,600
P Senior	69	70	70	76	285	3,600
L Nelson	73	67	74	72	286	3,110
J M Olazabal	73	69	71	73	286	3,110
T Kite	73	69	71	73	286	3,110
R Fehr	70	71	72	73	286	3,110
S Lyle	69	73	70	74	286	3,110
M Allen	73	70	75	69	287	2,800
J Sluman	74	69	72	72	287	2,800
B Crenshaw	70	70	73	74	287	2,800
D Hammond	73	70	68	76	287	2,800
M Standly	72	71	68	76	287	2,800
I Baker-Finch	73	69	70	76	288	2,650

AZINGER COMES OF AGE

A Commentary by Colin Callander

Paul Azinger isn't the world's most demonstrative player so when he danced around the green to celebrate his win in the USPGA Championship at Inverness it was clear he believed he'd done something rather special.

When, an hour later, he was still emotional enough to shed a tear or two in the ensuing press conference it was even more apparent that his win at Inverness meant a great deal to him. But then that wasn't altogether surprising as it was a moment he had waited a long time to savour.

Most of the leading Tour pros consider their careers incomplete without at least one Major title and Paul Azinger was no exception. He longed to see his name alongside Bobby Jones, Walter Hagen, Ben Hogan, Jack Nicklaus et al in the record books. He had grown tired of his label as The Best Player in the World Never to Have Won a Major and so when his time came it wasn't a surprise that he became so emotional.

In truth the only real surprise was that it took him quite so long to achieve it.

Paul Azinger first came to the fore when he finished the 1986 season in 29th place on the USPGA money list with more than $250,000 in official earnings but it was in the following year that he really made his mark. In America he won three titles, namely the Phoenix Open, the Las Vegas Invitational and the Canon Sammy Davis Jnr Greater Hartford Open to finish second on the money list with $822,481. It was a run of form which catapulted him up there alongside the world's best golfers and his reputation would have soared even higher still had it not been for his alarming collapse in the Open Championship at Muirfield in 1987.

It is evidence of the exulted place the Majors hold that until his win at Inverness, Azinger was best remembered (in Europe at least), not for the eight titles he had won on the US Tour (up to the start of the 1993 season) or, for that matter for his sterling performances in the Ryder Cup matches in 1989 and 1991, but for the moment of mental frailty which cost him the Muirfield Open and which in turn made Nick Faldo England's first Open champion since Tony Jacklin in 1969.

At Muirfield Azinger led the field by three shots with nine holes to go. He was still in front standing on the penultimate tee but then proceeded to drop shots on both the last two holes and to slip into a share of second place with Australia's Rodger Davis. He did earn £49,000 for his troubles, but at the same time also acquired a reputation for weakness under pressure.

As it transpired, it was a reputation which would haunt the American for the next six years and which wasn't banished completely until he won at Inverness. At the time Azinger told the world's media that his collapse wouldn't cause lasting damage but as time went on, and the 1980s became the 1990s, even he began to doubt his ability to win a major championship.

To the outsider, Azinger seemed to have no trouble at all shrugging off his Muirfield disappointment. In 1988 he did slip from 2nd to 11th on the US money list but still won the

Hertz Bay Hill Classic. In fact, he won at least once in America during each of the next four seasons and during that time never finished lower than 9th on the money list. It wasn't the sort of form which suggested that Azinger was struggling. On the surface all seemed well. But appearances can be deceptive.

Azinger now admits that his failure to win a Major was the one cloud in a career which had brought him more than $5 million in official US Tour earnings. He wasn't prepared to admit as much in public, however, at the beginning of 1993 season. On more than one occasion he pretended that it didn't matter to him that he hadn't won a Major but in his heart he knew that it did.

The records reveal that in the period between the Open at Muirfield and the start of the USPGA at Inverness in 1993, no fewer than 12 golfers succeeded in vaulting past Azinger and winning their first Major title. Azinger had his chances – most notably in the 1988 USPGA when he led after three rounds but lost out to Jeff Sluman – but he couldn't translate those chances into a win. Instead he had to watch and wonder as Sluman, Payne Stewart, Wayne Grady, John Daly and Nick Price won the USPGA title, as Ian Woosnam and Fred Couples won The Masters, as Curtis Strange, Tom Kite and Lee Janzen won the US Open and as Mark Calcavecchia and Ian Baker-Finch won the British Open.

It hurt. His family and friends told him it was only a matter of time before he joined them in the major league but he wasn't altogether sure. Each time he missed out on an opportunity his doubts grew. He started to dwell on his disappointments. He knew that he shouldn't, but it was becoming increasingly difficult to be positive when there wasn't much to be positive about. It hurt and the pain was getting worse.

Nor did it help that the media continued to call him The Best Golfer in the World Never to Win a Major. All that did was to remind him and the public of his failures and to increase the pressure on him.

Heading into the 1993 season Azinger was riddled with doubts but little by little he started to put those doubts into perspective and was aided in this by a run of results which convinced him that he had the ability and the temperament to win when pitted against the best.

His first mental boost had actually come at the end of 1992 when he overcame one of the year's strongest fields to capture the prestigious Tour Championship at Pinehurst in North Carolina. It isn't considered to be a Major but it was the next best thing and the manner in which he survived the challenge from golfers of the calibre of Corey Pavin, Lee Janzen, Fred Couples and Raymond Floyd gave him huge encouragement.

Azinger started 1993 on a high. He missed the cut at The Masters but wins in the Memorial Tournament and the New England Classic, plus a strong third place finish in the US Open at Baltusrol resurrected his confidence once more and brought him to Inverness in a good frame of mind. It was a mood he was to retain throughout the championship and in the end enable him to overcome everything that Greg Norman, Nick Faldo and the other leading challengers could throw at him.

'I've waited a long time for this,' an ecstatic Azinger said after he'd beaten Norman on the second extra hole of one of the most exciting Majors ever staged.

'I don't mind admitting that there were times when I doubted that I'd ever win a Major,' he added, with reference to the inner battle he'd had to overcome to achieve his dream. 'It means a lot and not least because of the way I've won it.'

3

THE RYDER CUP

RYDER CUP HISTORY

UNITED STATES 23, GREAT BRITAIN/EUROPE 5, TIES 2

1927	Worcester CC, Worcester, Mass.	US 9½, Britain 2½
1929	Moortown, Yorkshire, England	Britain 7, US 5
1931	Scioto CC, Columbus, Ohio	US 9, Britain 3
1933	Southport & Ainsdale, England	Britain 6 ½, US 5½
1935	Ridgewood CC, Ridgewood, NJ	US 9, Britain 3
1937	Southport & Ainsdale, England	US 8, Britain 4
	Ryder Cup not contested during World War II	
1947	Portland Golf Club, Portland, Ore	US 11, Britain 1
1949	Ganton GC, Scarborough, England	US 7, Britain 5
1951	Pinehurst CC, Pinehurst, NC	US 9½, Britain 2½
1953	Wentworth, Surrey, England	US 6½, Britain 5½
1955	Thunderbird Ranch & CC, Palm Springs, Ca.	US 8, Britain 4
1957	Lindrick GC, Yorkshire, England	Britain 7½, US 4½
1959	Eldorado CC, Palm Desert, Ca.	US 8½, Britain 3½
1961	Royal Lytham & St Anne's GC, St Anne's-on-the-Sea, England	US 14½, Britain 9½
1963	East Lake CC, Atlanta, Ga.	US 23, Britain 9
1965	Royal Birkdale GC, Southport, England	US 19½, Britain 12½
1967	Champions GC, Houston, Tex.	US 23½, Britain 8½
1969	Royal Birkdale GC, Southport, England	US 16, Britain 16 (TIE)
1971	Old Warson CC, St Louis, Mo.	US 18½, Britain 13½
1973	Muirfield, Scotland	US 18, Britain 13
1975	Laurel Valley GC, Ligonier, Pa.	US 21, Britain 11
1977	Royal Lytham & St Anne's GC, St Anne's-on-the-Sea, England	US 12½, Britain 7½
1979	The Greenbrier, White Sulphur Springs, W. Va.	US 17, Europe 11
1981	Walton Heath GC, Surrey, England	US 18½, Europe 9½
1983	PGA National GC, Palm Beach Gdns, Fla.	US 14½ Europe 13½
1985	The Belfry, Sutton Coldfield, England	Europe 16½, US 11½
1987	Muirfield Village, Ohio	Europe 15, US 13
1989	The Belfry, Sutton Coldfield, England	Europe 14, US 14 (TIE)
1991	Kiawah Island, South Carolina	US 14½, Europe 13½
1993	The Belfry, Sutton Coldfield, England	US 15, Europe 13

1993 Ryder Cup

The Belfry, Sutton Coldfield, England
September 24 - 26

Did you see that drive? Did you see those amazing recovery shots? Did you see the incredible hole-in-one? Did you see that putt? And did you see the expressions on their faces? The 30th Ryder Cup had it all.

Kiawah Island, or 'Pressure Cooker' Island as it became during the 1991 Ryder Cup, seemed an impossible act to follow. Two years on it still appeared unreal: that spectacular course off the coast of South Carolina – that spectacularly difficult course – with its emerald fairways and its island greens floating in seas of sand and scrub; the ghostly silence as Bernhard Langer crouched over a slippery six foot putt on the final hole, needing to sink it to retain the trophy for Europe. Another world.

The Belfry is situated on the suburban fringes of Birmingham, close to the industrial heart of England. Although immaculately groomed, it will never win a beauty contest and when day broke on the first morning of the 1993 Ryder Cup the course was imprisoned in a blanket of fog. It was an inauspicious start and caused play to be delayed for two and a half hours. But from the moment the fog lifted, allowing Corey Pavin to strike the opening drive – through the times of those amazing recovery shots of Seve Ballesteros and Nick Faldo's incredible hole-in-one and on to the final putt by Paul Azinger – it was an immensely absorbing contest.

There were many occasions, in fact, when the 30th Ryder Cup surpassed the 29th, both as a golfing spectacle and, especially perhaps, in providing an example to the watching world of good sportsmanship. There was a noticeably greater camaraderie between the players and a better atmosphere off the fairways (among the galleries, for instance). The final day didn't bring quite as sensational an ending as the Sunday at Kiawah Island (which is hardly surprising) but it was still sufficiently exciting for the fingernails of armchair viewers on both sides of the Atlantic to be seriously chewed.

Early morning fog delays the start of play

The two teams were as evenly matched on paper as they proved to be in practice. The European side included golfers from seven different countries, with Joakim Haeggman (one of captain Bernard Gallacher's three 'Wild Card' selections) and Costantino Rocca becoming Sweden and Italy's first ever representatives.

The other rookies appearing at The Belfry were, for Europe, England's Barry Lane and

Corey Pavin starred for America on Day One

Peter Baker and for the United States, Lee Janzen, Davis Love, John Cook and Jim Gallagher – four rookies each, in other words.

In the two years since Kiawah Island it is fair to say that Europe's top four players had been Faldo, Langer, Woosnam and Montgomerie and that their counterparts on the American side were Couples, Azinger, Kite and Stewart. As for the Captains' selections, there was a wonderful contrast in personalities with the mercurial Spaniards (Ballesteros and Olazabal) on the one hand and the gutsy, veteran Americans (Ray Floyd and Lanny Wadkins) on the other.

Both teams then, could claim to have a nice blend of youth and experience and each was liberally sprinkled with Major winners and leading moneywinners. Perhaps the most vital question on the eve of the great match concerned how well the inspirational partnership of Ballesteros and Olazabal would perform. Neither golfer could be particularly proud of his achievements in 1993. 'Proud'? Perhaps that was the key: pride means everything to the Spanish and the greater the occasion the greater the pride.

But back to Corey Pavin, whom we left driving off at the still slightly foggy first hole. The format for the first two days of the Ryder Cup provides for four foursomes matches in the morning followed by four fourball matches in the afternoon. Watson had decided to partner Pavin with Wadkins on the first morning and it proved to be one of his best decisions of the week. The Americans gelled immediately and proved too strong for their opponents, Mark James and Sam Torrance. Watson invited Wadkins and Pavin to repeat their efforts in the afternoon and they duly obliged by collecting a second point by defeating Bernhard Langer and Barry Lane.

Fortunately for Bernard Gallacher and his men, not all the Americans were playing as well as Pavin and Wadkins. The morning foursomes were shared two points apiece. Tom Kite and Davis Love gained the other American point when they became the first ever team to defeat Ballesteros and Olazabal in a foursomes match. The decisive stroke in their 2 & 1 victory – and it was unquestionably the shot of the day – occurred when Tom Kite carried his three-wood tee-shot over the water and onto the green at the short par four 10th, after watching the Spaniards elect to lay up short of the hazard. Love holed the putt for an eagle two.

Europe's points in the foursomes came from the strong pairing of Nick Faldo and Colin Montgomerie, who beat Fred Couples and Ray Floyd and from Ian Woosnam and Bernhard Langer who inflicted a 7 & 5 defeat on Paul Azinger and Payne Stewart. So, it was 'honours even' in the morning, but in the afternoon Europe edged ahead.

Pavin and Wadkins, as mentioned, won their fourball clash with Langer and Lane fairly comfortably but in the other three games American golfers ran into a storm of European birdies. The first match after lunch saw the introduction of the Ian Woosnam - Peter Baker partnership. As the much more experienced of the two, Woosnam was expected to play the principal role, whereas in fact, to use his words, he simply 'strolled around all afternoon' as his young partner performed magnificently, firing six birdies, including a 20 foot winning putt at the final hole to beat a stunned Lee Janzen and Jim Gallagher.

Ballesteros and Olazabal were given an immediate opportunity to avenge their foursomes defeat when they were drawn to play a second game against Kite and Love. The Americans played about as well as they did in the morning; their problem, however, was that a fourball pairing of Nicklaus and Palmer at their peak would have been pushed to live with the Spaniards on Friday afternoon. When the match ended after 15 holes Ballesteros and Olazabal had a better ball score of 11 under par. Did somebody mention the word 'pride'?

An equally fascinating and closer encounter was taking place between Faldo and

Ian Woosnam and Peter Baker celebrate at the 18th as Baker sinks a 20 foot winning putt

Montgomerie and Azinger and Couples. Faldo was in tremendous form, scoring seven birdies and twice chipping-in from off the green. 'Monty' supported him well but the Americans were able to counter everything that their opponents threw at them. The game was all-square after 17 holes when poor visibility forced a suspension of play (it was 7:15pm and the street lights had been illuminated for some time!) The overall match score now

Battling Europeans: (far left) José-Maria Olazabal and (left) Colin Montgomerie and Nick Faldo

stood at 4-3 to Europe but with one game still to complete the Americans had a chance to draw level.

It had been a riveting opening day, one which Tom Watson neatly summarised when he said, 'the competition was so intense you could have written a novel about it.'

We didn't have to wait much more than twelve hours before the drama began to unfold once again. At 8:00am on Saturday Faldo and company teed off at the 18th hole to complete their unfinished business and at about 8:20am the Englishman rolled in a twelve foot putt to halve the match and make the score 4½ - 3½ to Europe.

It was a marvellous pressure-putt and

provided the perfect tonic for Faldo and Montgomerie, who walked immediately from the 18th green to the 1st tee where they were due to lead-off for Europe in Saturday's foursomes. Their opponents on this occasion were America's success story of the first day, the unbeaten team of Pavin and Wadkins. As expected, it was a close match, but following another of those famous Faldo chip-ins, this time for a two at the 14th, the British duo went on to win by 3 & 2.

Things were beginning to look rather good for Bernard Gallacher. Behind Faldo and Montgomerie, only the rookie pairing of Baker and Lane was failing to deliver – the combined experience of Floyd and Stewart proving too much – but Langer and Woosnam claimed the important scalp of Couples and Azinger and the Spaniards, matched incredibly for a third time against Kite and Love, brought Europe into lunch with a handsome 7½ - 4½ lead.

The Americans were probably more perplexed than anything else. For a day and a half they believed they had played as well as Europe yet were now trailing by three points. Kite and Love's 2 & 1 defeat at the hands of Ballesteros and Olazabal was the hardest loss to comprehend. It is a fact that not one of Seve's drives finished on the fairway! Of course the Spaniards scrambled with all the skill and flair that has become their trademark, but to Kite and Love it must have seemed like an old-fashioned mugging.

(Above)
Paul Azinger played superbly without scoring too many points.
(Left)
The Spanish magician: Seve tries to conjure something from nothing

If the Ryder Cup was not to slip from their grasp, it was imperative that America should win the afternoon fourball series. If the points were halved, for instance, Europe would need to win only five of the 12 singles points on Sunday.

Such a scenario, of course, didn't happen. Watson's team rose to the occasion and rallied magnificently on Saturday afternoon. With hindsight it isn't difficult to identify this moment as the turning point in the contest; somewhat controversially (see John Hopkins' Commentary on page 86) Gallacher rested Langer and Ballesteros and, whilst we may never know what was discussed at the American table that lunchtime, it was certainly an inspired and remarkably determined team that emerged for those crucial fourballs.

A Swedish triumph and an Italian tragedy: contrasting images from the final day of the 1993 Ryder Cup

The unlikely heroes of the hour were John Cook and Chip Beck – 'unlikely' as this was a first appearance in the match for both of them and they defeated the seemingly invincible team of Faldo and Montgomerie. Pavin and Gallagher overwhelmed James and Rocca 5 &

4 and Floyd and Stewart successfully parried a spirited, if belated thrust from Olazabal and Haeggman. Only Woosnam and Baker (or to be more precise, only Baker's magical putting) prevented an American clean sweep.

So, 8½ - 7½ – things were looking rather better for Tom Watson. Europe still lead, of course, but it was now by the most slender of margins and Watson (and Gallacher) knew that American teams invariably perform well in the singles. As dusk enveloped The Belfry on Saturday evening, the phrase on everyone's lips was, 'Beware America's strength in depth.'

Ryder Cup Sunday: is there a comparable occasion? Everything to play for – and everything to lose; a continent's golfing reputation at stake. It appears to have grown that important.

If strength in depth was reckoned to be America's greatest asset going into the singles, Europe's best chance was thought to rest on the performances of its 'big six': Faldo, Langer, Woosnam, Ballesteros, Olazabal and Montgomerie. So far it was they, together with the revelational Peter Baker who had secured all of Europe's points. Six more were required for a home victory; America needed six and a half to retain the Cup and seven for an outright win. What happened? Between them, Europe's 'big six' managed to win just one and a half points. Only Montgomerie won his match (1 up against Lee Janzen) and Woosnam and Faldo halved their games with Couples and Azinger respectively. As for the others, Langer was beaten comprehensively by Tom Kite, an out-of-sorts Ballesteros was crushed by Jim Gallagher and Olazabal lost to 'Old Man' Floyd.

Davis Love wins a vital point for America after defeating Costantino Rocca (opposite) on the final green

Fifteen points and thirteen smiles: Tom Watson and his team keep their hands on the trophy

A poor showing from Europe's elite? Yes and no: the truth of the matter is that the Americans' golf was consistently good and occasionally brilliant. Only Seve played badly; 'I never thought a Gallagher would beat a Ballesteros', said his conqueror, but then no one expected to see the Spaniard take 42 strokes on the front nine either. 51 year-old Floyd was four under par when he defeated 27 year-old Olazabal, while Kite, who played the 8th to the 11th holes in birdie-birdie-eagle-birdie was six under par at the conclusion of his match with Langer.

The fact that Europe came within a few putts of winning the 30th Ryder Cup speaks volumes for the performances of the 'lesser lights', particularly the rookies on its team. Of the matches on Sunday (and there were only 11 in total when the injured Torrance and his nominal partner Wadkins had to withdraw) eight went all the way to the 18th hole. At one stage it seemed a possibilty that all four of Europe's rookies might win their games. Both Haeggman and Baker did but Rocca, after missing a three foot putt to win his match on the 17th, and Lane, who let slip a lead of three up with five to play, were both beaten on the last green. Ironically it was an American rookie, Davis Love, who holed the decisive putt for America when he defeated the unfortunate Rocca.

Love's win gave America its 14th point, thus ensuring that the trophy had been retained. At that instant there was a slight chance that Europe could still tie the match as the games involving Olazabal and Floyd and Faldo and Azinger had still to be resolved.

Faldo was ahead in his game for much of the afternoon, helped in no small way, of course, by an extraordinary hole-in-one at the 14th (only the second in Ryder Cup history). Olazabal was three down with four to play against Floyd but fought back to one down after winning the 15th and 17th holes; all was lost for Europe, however, when the Spaniard's drive at the 18th met a watery grave. Faldo and Azinger played on to the finish and the American appropriately concluded matters with a marvellous birdie putt to square the match on the final green. A half for Azinger but a victory for the United States. Strength and depth had won the day.

THE 30TH RYDER CUP

24 - 26 September 1993 · The Belfry

EUROPE	Points	USA	Points
Foursomes: Morning			
S Torrance & M James	0	L Wadkins & C Pavin (4 & 3)	1
I Woosnam & B Langer (7 & 5)	1	P Azinger & P Stewart	0
S Ballesteros & J M Olazabal	0	T Kite & D Love III (2 & 1)	1
N Faldo & C Montgomerie (4 & 3)	1	R Floyd & F Couples	0
Fourballs: Afternoon			
I Woosnam & P Baker (1 hole)	1	J Gallagher Jnr & L Janzen	0
B Langer & B Lane	0	L Wadkins & C Pavin (4 & 2)	1
N Faldo & C Montgomerie (halved)	½	P Azinger & F Couples (halved)	½
S Ballesteros & J M Olazabal (4 & 3)	1	D Love III & T Kite	0
Foursomes: Morning			
N Faldo & C Montgomerie (3 & 2)	1	L Wadkins & C Pavin	0
B Langer & I Woosnam (2 & 1)	1	F Couples & P Azinger	0
P Baker & B Lane	0	R Floyd & P Stewart (3 & 2)	1
S Ballesteros & J M Olazabal (2 & 1)	1	D Love III & T Kite	0
Fourballs: Afternoon			
N Faldo & C Montgomerie	0	J Cook & C Beck (2 holes)	1
M James & C Rocca	0	C Pavin & J Gallagher Jnr (5 & 4)	1
I Woosnam & P Baker (6 & 5)	1	F Couples & P Azinger	0
J M Olazabal & J Haeggman	0	R Floyd & P Stewart (2 & 1)	1
Singles:			
S Torrance (halved)*	½	L Wadkins (halved)	½
I Woosnam (halved)	½	F Couples (halved)	½
B Lane	0	C Beck (1 hole)	1
C Montgomerie (1 hole)	1	L Janzen	0
P Baker (2 holes)	1	C Pavin	0
J Haeggman (1 hole)	1	J Cook	0
M James	0	P Stewart (3 & 2)	1
C Rocca	0	D Love III (1hole)	1
S Ballesteros	0	J Gallagher Jnr (3 & 2)	1
J M Olazabal	0	R Floyd (2 holes)	1
B Langer	0	T Kite (5 & 3)	1
N Faldo (halved)	½	P Azinger (halved)	½
	EUROPE 13		**USA 15**

* Torrance withdrawn injured

THE RYDER CUP IN RETROSPECT

A Commentary by John Hopkins

There is evidence to indicate that some golfers were not consumed with interest in the 30th Ryder Cup. A band of American amateurs chose to travel to Europe and play at Machrihanish rather than follow events at The Belfry and there was a cricket match between the Antipodean professionals and caddies that same week.

But everyone else, or so it seemed, had eyes only for what unfolded at The Belfry on those three days in September. More than 60 countries around the world received the BBC TV pictures, which just goes to show this was no ordinary Ryder Cup. There is no such thing as an ordinary Ryder Cup any more. The last ordinary Ryder Cup was in 1981 when the Americans routed Europe on a blasted (Walton) heath in Surrey. In 1983 Europe gave the US a fright by nearly winning. In 1985 and 1987 Europe did win. In 1989 came that famous tie and in 1991, well, if you need to be reminded what happened in 1991 then you've clearly not been paying attention. The US won by one point.

This Ryder Cup was the most important there had ever been. Why? Let Seve Ballesteros, the most dominant figure in European golf since Harry Vardon in the Edwardian era, explain. 'We are playing for our national pride' Ballesteros said. 'We are playing for the supremacy of the game. It is the best competition in golf, including the majors. It brings more attention than any other competition.'

So when all the dust had settled on Sunday evening and the US had retained Sam Ryder's Trophy, what had been learned? A lot actually. Here are six lessons to be borne in mind as preparations begin for the 31st Ryder Cup, which will be held at Oak Hill Country Club, Rochester, New York, in September 1995.

1) It was the end of an era for European golf. The era had begun on a July afternoon in 1969 when Tony Jacklin won the Open and followed this up 11 months later by taking the US Open as well. He laid the foundations for European golf. Seve Ballesteros burst on to the scene in 1976 and then came Bernhard Langer. By 1983 the European Ryder Cup team of four Scots, four Englishmen, two Spaniards, a Welshman and a West German came within one point of an historic first victory on American soil. In 1985 Langer won the US Masters, Sandy Lyle the Open and Europe the Ryder Cup. Faldo won the Open in 1987, as he was to again in 1990 and 1992 and in between he won the 1989 and 1990 US Masters. Ballesteros took the 1988 Open, Woosnam won at Augusta in 1991.

All those triumphs are over, now. The cheers have died away. It is stretching the bounds of possibility to breaking point to consider these major championship winners capable of bringing home even half as many major titles in the next few years as they have in the past. None is under 35.

2) The Ryder Cup confirmed that the US has regained dominance in golf. At the year's end, the US held the Ryder, Walker, Curtis, World and Dunhill Cups – and Corey Pavin was the World Matchplay champion, the first such American since Bill Rogers in 1979.

3) There is an art to captaincy. You don't just let the players decide it themselves. That is chairmanship by committee not captaincy. Tom Watson described himself as a captain by consensus. He certainly spoke a lot to all his players, was wonderfully attentive to their needs but was firm when he had to be.

The key moments of this Ryder Cup came late on Saturday morning when Bernard Gallacher allowed Langer and Ballesteros to withdraw from the afternoon's fourballs. After lunch Olazabal was paired with Joakim Haeggman and lost a match that he and Ballesteros might have won. At lunchtime, the US trailed 4½ – 7½; by tea-time they had closed to within one point.

Gallacher was wrong to allow these two players to rest. It was a test of his captaincy and though he passed most other tests I think he failed this one. 'I am a great believer in players knowing their best' Gallacher said. 'I am not clever enough to make players do things against their will. Some captains can but I can't. I could see that Seve was struggling and Bernhard said he felt he was too short a hitter to be of any use in four balls and it was better to use some of the younger guys.'

This was what stuck in Tony Jacklin's craw. The man who had led Europe so successfully from 1983 until handing over to Gallacher for the 1991 match did not think that his successor should have allowed Ballesteros and Langer to withdraw from Saturday's fourballs. He regarded that as an abrogation of responsibility. He had sweet talked Ballesteros into doing what he, Jacklin, wanted and not what he, Ballesteros, wanted to and he could not understand why Gallacher could not have done the same thing.

There is a degree of harshness in condemning Gallacher's captaincy on the basis of what happened on Saturday afternoon but I am afraid such is life. Had Europe won, he would have been acclaimed as a hero, a brilliant man manager, a tactician par excellence. Because they lost, he cannot expect to be absolved.

4) Another lesson for Oak Hill, 1995, is that the Europeans traditionally do poorly in the singles. It might be fairer to say that the Americans wax strong when they're playing on their own while too many Europeans wane. Take Ray Floyd as an example. The oldest man to appear in a Ryder Cup, he had played three matches out of four prior to the singles. This was at odds with the widely-held view before the start that he would be used sparingly.

On Saturday he played twice and he was the last man to leave the practice ground that evening. On Sunday he gunned down José-Maria Olazabal in a blaze of birdies and eagles making light of the fact that he was, as near as no matter twice Olazabal's age.

One stark fact: the Americans have lost the singles only once since the 1950s.

5) There will not be a mix-up over the signing of menus at Rochester. Tom Watson's gaffe came at a dinner on the Tuesday night when he ordered his men not to sign autographs, which led to Sam Torrance being snubbed. That was a mistake (Watson's word) but it was his only one of the week. No sooner had Lanny Wadkins been confirmed as the American captain for Oak Hill than he said he intended to talk to Bernhard Gallacher about that very subject.

6) Seve Ballesteros is in a deep slump and may have to alter his swing, which is still that of a young man, and cut down on his schedule to get out of it. He wants to represent Europe in 1995 when there will be only two wild card selections and ten players will be chosen from the Ryder Cup points table. A European team without Ballesteros sounds funny doesn't it? It would be the first since 1981 if it did happen.

4

Heineken World Cup

Heineken World Cup

ROLL · OF · HONOUR

1953 Argentina	Roberto de Vicenzo	Antonio Cerda	Beaconsfield GC, Montreal, Canada
1954 Australia	Peter Thomson	Kel Nagle	Laval-sur-le-Lac GC, Montreal, Canada
1955 United States	Ed Furgol	Chick Harbert	Columbia GC, Washington DC, USA
1956 United States	Ben Hogan	Sam Snead	Wentworth Club, Surrey, England
1957 Japan	T Nakamura	Koichi Ono	Kasumigaseki CC, Tokyo, Japan
1958 Ireland	Harry Bradshaw	Christy O'Connor	Club de Golf Mexico, Mexico
1959 Australia	Peter Thomson	Kel Nagle	Royal Melbourne GC, Melbourne, Australia
1960 United States	Arnold Palmer	Sam Snead	Portmarnock GC, Dublin, Ireland
1961 United States	Sam Snead	Jimmy Demaret	Dorado Beach GC, Dorado Beach, Puerto Rico
1962 United States	Arnold Palmer	Sam Snead	Jockey Club Golf, Buenos Aires, Argentina
1963 United States	Jack Nicklaus	Arnold Palmer	Golf de St-Nom-la-Breteche, Paris, France
1964 United States	Jack Nicklaus	Arnold Palmer	Royal Kaanapali GC, Maui, Hawaii
1965 South Africa	Gary Player	Harold Henning	RACE del Club de Campo, Madrid, Spain
1966 United States	Jack Nicklaus	Arnold Palmer	Tokyo Yomiuri CC, Tokyo, Japan
1967 United States	Jack Nicklaus	Arnold Palmer	Club de Golf Mexico, Mexico City, Mexico
1968 Canada	Al Balding	George Knudson	Circolo Golf Olgiata, Rome, Italy
1969 United States	Lee Trevino	Orville Moody	Singapore Island CC, Singapore
1970 Australia	David Graham	Bruce Devlin	Jockey Club Golf, Buenos Aires, Argentina
1971 United States	Jack Nicklaus	Lee Trevino	PGA National GC, Palm Beach, Florida, USA

The spectacular 18th hole at Lake Nona

1972 Republic of China	Hsieh Min-Nan	Lu Liang-Huan	Royal Melbourne GC, Melbourne, Australia
1973 United States	Johnny Miller	Jack Nicklaus	Golf Nueva Andalucia, Marbella, Spain
1974 South Africa	Bobby Cole	Dale Hayes	Lagunita CC, Caracus, Venezuela
1975 United States	Johnny Miller	Lou Graham	Navatanee GC, Bangkok, Thailand
1976 Spain	Manuel Pinero	Seve Ballesteros	Mission Hills CC, Rancho Mirage, California, USA
1977 Spain	Antonio Garrido	Seve Ballesteros	Wack Wack G & CC, Manila, Philippines
1978 United States	John Mahaffey	Andy North	Princeville Makai GC, Kauai, Hawaii
1979 United States	John Mahaffey	Hale Irwin	Glyfada GC, Athens, Greece
1980 Canada	Dan Halldorson	Jim Nelford	El Rincon Club, Bogota, Columbia
1981 No Tournament			
1982 Spain	Manuel Pinero	José-Maria Canizares	Pierre Marques GC, Acapulco, Mexico
1983 United States	Rex Caldwell	John Cook	Pondok Indah GC, Jakarta, Indonesia
1984 Spain	José-Maria Canizares	Jose Rivero	Olgiata GC, Rome, Italy
1985 Canada	Dave Barr	Dan Halldorson	La Quinta GC, California, USA
1986 No Tournament			
1987 Wales	Ian Woosnam	David Llewellyn	Kapalua Bay GC, Maui, Hawaii
1988 United States	Ben Crenshaw	Mark McCumber	Royal Melbourne GC, Melbourne, Australia
1989 Australia	Peter Fowler	Wayne Grady	Club de Golf Las Brisas, Marbella, Spain
1990 Germany	Bernhard Langer	Torsten Giedeon	Grand Cypress Resort, Florida, USA
1991 Sweden	Per-Ulrik Johansson	Anders Forsbrand	La Querce GC, Rome, Italy
1992 United States	Fred Couples	Davis Love III	La Moraleja, Madrid, Spain
1993 United States	Fred Couples	Davis Love III	Lake Nona, Florida, USA

INTERNATIONAL · TROPHY

(Leading Individual Player)

1953	Antonio Cerda	Argentina
1954	Stan Leonard	Canada
1955	Ed Furgol	United States
1956	Ben Hogan	United States
1957	Torakichi Nakamura	Japan
1958	Angel Miguel	Spain
1959	Stan Leonard	Canada
1960	Flory Van Donck	Belgium
1961	Sam Snead	United States
1962	Roberto de Vicenzo	Argentina
1963	Jack Nicklaus	United States
1964	Jack Nicklaus	United States
1965	Gary Player	South Africa
1966	George Knudson	Canada
1967	Arnold Palmer	United States
1968	Al Balding	Canada
1969	Lee Trevino	United States
1970	Roberto de Vicenzo	Argentina
1971	Jack Nicklaus	United States
1972	Hsieh Min-Nan	Rep. of China
1973	Johnny Miller	United States
1974	Bobby Cole	South Africa
1975	Johnny Miller	United States
1976	Ernesto Acosta	Mexico
1977	Gary Player	South Africa
1978	John Mahaffey	United States
1979	Hale Irwin	United States
1980	Sandy Lyle	Scotland
1981	No Tournament	
1982	Manuel Pinero	Spain
1983	Dave Barr	Canada
1984	José-Maria Canizares	Spain
1985	Howard Clark	England
1986	No Tournament	
1987	Ian Woosnam	Wales
1988	Ben Crenshaw	United States
1989	Peter Fowler	Australia
1990	Payne Stewart	United States
1991	Ian Woosnam	Wales
1992	Brett Ogle	Australia
1993	Bernhard Langer	Germany

Bernhard Langer, winner of the International Trophy in 1993

1993 Heineken World Cup Golf

Lake Nona, Orlando, Florida, November 11-14

In last year's *Heineken World of Golf* we left the so called 'Dream Team' of Couples and Love jetting off into the sunset, having plundered much Spanish gold in a thrilling 38th World Cup at La Moraleja. Twelve months on and a continent away, as the sun rose over the magnificent setting of Lake Nona in Florida our heroes had returned. The 39th (and now Heineken sponsored) World Cup was being staged at one of the best golf courses in America and the reigning champions, Fred and Davis, were back to defend their title. And they were in tremendous form: the previous week Couples had won the Kapalua International event in Hawaii and Love had finished third. Both had played significant roles in helping America retain the Ryder Cup in September and in October, a fortnight after Couples was guiding the US to success in the Dunhill Cup at St Andrews (he was easily the strongman of the team) Love was winning a tournament in Las Vegas by eight strokes. Who, or what, could possibly stop them from winning at Lake Nona – in their own backyard? Actually, several teams were very capable, moreover, history wasn't entirely on America's side.

Come to mention it, whose 'backyard' was it anyway? The team that everybody expected to make a strong challenge was Zimbabwe.

Robert Allenby of Australia (left) and Jean Van de Velde of France

Fred Couples drives at Lake Nona

Nick Price (the US Tour's leading moneywinner in 1993) and Mark McNulty (winner of the 1992-93 South African Order of Merit) were its representatives. Not only were they two exceptional players, but Lake Nona just happened to be Orlando resident Price's 'home course' and McNulty had played it several times when visiting his lifelong friend; by contrast, the subtle – though extremely fair – challenges of Lake Nona were a total mystery to the American pair prior to their defence. Of previous champions, only the formidable team of Jack Nicklaus and Arnold Palmer had successfully defended golf's oldest team trophy, and that was in the days when fewer countries could field strong sides – imagine Germany and Sweden, the champions of 1990 and 1991, winning in the 60s.

The majority of the teams at Lake Nona comprised their nations' top two players. Nick Faldo was a notable absentee from the English side, although he fully intended to play before a wrist injury forced his late withdrawal. The likes of Bernhard Langer, Ian Woosnam, Ernie Els, Colin Montgomerie, Rodger Davis and Ronan Rafferty were in Florida, competing not only for the team prize but also for the coveted International Trophy, awarded to the player achieving the lowest individual score.

While it is fair to say that some teams were never likely to win at Lake Nona – a quick glance at the final aggregate totals of Jamaica and Israel, for instance, indicates as much – the guiding philosophy behind the event is always worth repeating: 'to spread fellowship and goodwill among the nations of the world'. Presumably someone in authority explained this to the famous Lake Nona alligators.

Lake Nona's secret police usually keep a low profile

Warm sunshine, blue skies and cottonwool clouds greeted the players on Thursday. It was a glorious morning: Lake Nona never looked better, with its green ribbon fairways weaving their way between towering pine trees and vast stretches of dazzling white sand.

It was a perfect picture of peace, until Fred Couples shattered the serenity by hitting a two-iron 250 yards straight into the hole for a two at the 532 yards par five 9th. It was an astonishing shot – the first ever albatross (or double-eagle) of Fred's life. Up until that point

the Americans had been ambling along, doing nothing special, and France were the surprise early leaders of the tournament. Jean Van de Velde was the player shooting all the birdies. He made seven in total and finished his opening round with a six under par 66. Van de Velde's problem was that his team mate Marc Farry was struggling to a 74. Couples' albatross helped him to match the Frenchman's 66, a score which, rather ominously, was the same as his first round at La Moraleja. Davis Love returned a 71 and with a team total of 137 (seven under par), the USA eased to the top of the leaderboard. At the end of the first day the host nation enjoyed a three shot lead over France and South Africa, with Zimbabwe four behind.

Nothing much went right (or wrong) for Nick Price and Mark McNulty on Thursday, but both certainly stepped up a gear on Friday with McNulty scoring a joint best-of-the-day 68 and Price a 69. With the help of an eagle at the 11th, Love was able to match Price's score but the best that his partner Couples could manage was a 71, this despite his own eagle at the par four 14th. No other teams made significant progress in the second round, although with Robert Allenby scoring a 68 and Rodger Davis a 70, Australia moved into third place. Zimbabwe had cut America's lead to a single stroke and in the 'tournament within a tournament' Van de Velde also held a one shot advantage at the halfway stage, his 136 total (eight under par) being one better than Couples, Torrance and Langer.

An albatross and a pair of eagles already: somebody was unleashing some mighty hits. Both Couples and Love are, of course, renowned long hitters; Fred's nickname isn't 'Boom Boom' for nothing and his eagle at the 309 yards 14th came as a result of his driving the green (as it happens Messrs Price and McNulty were putting at the time – but that's another story!) When he wants to, Love can propel the ball even further – as in the third round when his drive at the 358 yards 5th left him with just a 'flick' to the green.

Mark McNulty of Zimbabwe

The Americans' extra distance proved a crucial asset when they confronted the Zimbabwean challenge head on, on Saturday. For much of the round it was a very close contest and the Americans' length countered their opponents' generally greater accuracy. The modest scoring – Couples had a 70, Price and Love a 71 and McNulty a 72 – might suggest that the four played fairly conservatively, especially as they failed to pull away from the pursuing pack, but this certainly wasn't the case. Couples, for instance, had a real rollercoaster of a day: his 70 was made up of five bogeys, six pars and seven birdies. And the reason that Price didn't score a 66 or 67 was that he missed a succession of birdie putts from between 5 and 15 feet.

Scotland's Sam Torrance and Colin Montgomerie

So, what of the 'pursuing pack'? The Australians continued to cling to the leaders' coat tails but they were joined on Saturday by Scotland, in the form of Colin Montgomerie and Sam Torrance who had also been 'hovering in the background' for three days and, more surprisingly, by a rampaging New Zealand. Lying 12 shots behind Couples and Love after 36 holes, Frank Nobilo scored a very useful 69 while his Kiwi colleague Greg Turner played superbly, firing eight birdies in a round of 64. After three rounds Australia, Scotland and New Zealand had closed to within one of second placed Zimbabwe, who in turn were three behind the Americans: five teams separated by just four shots.

If the main contest now had the potential to develop into a close finish, the destination of the individual prize could be predicted with some certainty on the eve of the final round. Bernhard Langer was the reason. Although his team-mate, Sven Struver, was playing poorly, Langer had apparently rediscovered his Masters touch. A 69 on Thursday had been followed by a 68 on Friday and now on Saturday he scored an excellent 66. With Couples producing that rollercoaster 70 and Van de Velde and Torrance both taking 71 it gave him a four shot lead – the same margin that he had taken into the final round at Augusta in April. (In fact, Langer returned a 69 on Sunday for an extremely impressive (or 'unbelievable' as Price described it) total of 16 under par and a comfortable three shot victory).

The blue skies and the cottonwool clouds returned for the final round (Saturday had been a humid, US Open-type of day), and it was fairly hot. It certainly wasn't a typical Scottish November day, and sadly for Sam and 'Monty' it wasn't to be famous Scottish day either. Three dropped strokes early in the final round effectively ended their challenge before it could ever gain momentum, although they did rally later in the day to finish third. Australia and New Zealand were paired together on Sunday: could their great rivalry inspire an antipodean success? Again, unfortunately not. After his 64 on Saturday Turner shot a 75 on Sunday and with Rodger

Mission complete: Couples and Love retain the Heineken World Cup for America

Davis scoring 74, and neither of their partners breaking 70, the centre stage was left to America and Zimbabwe.

Good fortune alone never decided the outcome of a major event; Fred Couples didn't win the 1992 Masters just because his ball seemingly defied Sir Isaac Newton's theories at the 12th hole, when it somehow failed to roll down a steep bank into Rae's Creek – he played some tremendous golf as well. What luck there was at Lake Nona, however, did seem to go America's (or at least Couples') way. The albatross was one obvious example and another occurred in the final round at the 1st hole, when a thinned chip-shot by Couples crashed into the pin and bolted into the cup for a birdie. It was extremely timely to say the least; it set the Americans on their way and Price and McNulty could never quite catch up. They threatened to do so on more than one occasion, however, during an afternoon of fine golf, but over the closing stretch the defending champions pulled away and eventually won by a margin of five strokes.

Too long, too strong and when it mattered most, too 'on song'; Couples and Love had retained the Heineken World Cup for America, emulating the great achievements of Nicklaus and Palmer. As at La Moraleja, Fred and Davis had come, seen and conquered and once again were jetting off into the sunset with the spoils of victory.

1993 HEINEKEN WORLD CUP GOLF

FINAL · SCORES

USA	**556**					
F Couples	66	71	70	68	275	
D Love III	71	69	71	70	281	$130,000 each
ZIMBABWE	**561**					
N Price	70	69	71	68	278	
M McNulty	71	68	72	72	283	75,000 each
SCOTLAND	**565**					
S Torrance	68	69	71	73	281	
C Montgomerie	75	70	69	70	284	50,000 each
AUSTRALIA	**566**					
R Allenby	72	68	70	70	280	
R Davis	70	70	72	74	286	37,500 each
SPAIN	**567**					
M A Jimenez	72	70	72	68	282	
J Rivero	73	72	66	74	285	30,000 each
SOUTH AFRICA	**567**					
E Els	69	71	72	66	278	
R Goosen	71	74	69	76	290	30,000 each
NEW ZEALAND	**568**					
F Nobilo	74	69	69	71	283	
G Turner	73	73	64	75	285	18,750 each
GERMANY	**571**					
B Langer	69	68	66	69	272	
S Struver	74	75	74	76	299	12,500 each
IRELAND	**573**					
R Rafferty	71	69	73	71	284	
P McGinley	72	71	73	73	289	9,250 each
ITALY	**573**					
C Rocca	71	75	67	70	283	
S Grappasonni	74	72	69	75	290	9,250 each
ENGLAND	**574**					
D Gilford	69	73	72	72	286	
M James	76	74	68	70	288	7,000 each
CANADA	**574**					
D Barr	74	70	70	71	285	
R Zokol	76	71	70	72	289	7,000 each
SWEDEN	**575**					
A Forsbrand	71	69	74	68	282	
J Haeggman	72	77	72	72	293	5,250 each
FRANCE	**575**					
J Van de Velde	66	70	71	72	279	
M-A Farry	74	78	72	72	296	5,250 each
PARAGUAY	**579**					
P R Martinez	74	73	69	71	287	
F R Franco	73	73	69	77	292	4,500 each
WALES	**582**					
M Mouland	68	70	75	73	286	
I Woosnam	74	79	74	69	296	4,000 each
BRAZIL	**583**					
A Barcellos	76	70	70	71	287	
J Corteiz	75	70	75	76	296	3,500 each
JAPAN	**588**					
T Katsuyoshi	74	73	72	73	292	
H Shigenobu	70	77	76	73	296	3,500 each
ARGENTINA	**592**					
E Romero	71	70	72	75	288	
L Carbonetti	73	80	77	74	304	3,500 each
HONG KONG	**592**					
R Kan	74	72	75	76	297	
Y S Ming	73	74	76	77	300	3,500 each

MEXICO	**597**					
R Cazaubon	68	79	75	76	298	
E Serna	78	75	72	74	299	3,500 each
NETHERLANDS	**602**					
C Van Der Velde	74	72	73	77	296	
C Van Waesberghe	78	75	75	74	302	3,500 each
GREECE	**603**					
G Nikitaides	77	75	73	75	300	
V Karatzias	74	75	79	75	303	3,500 each
TAIWAN	**609**					
Y-S Hsieh	76	72	76	77	301	
L-H Chen	80	78	79	71	308	3,500 each
BERMUDA	**617**					
K Swan	76	76	72	79	303	
D Pearman	78	79	76	81	314	3,500 each
PUERTO RICO	**629**					
R Castrillo	78	77	76	77	308	
J Rodriguez	85	77	77	82	321	3,500 each
FIJI	**646**					
D Prakash	80	79	74	81	314	
V Kalou	89	79	82	82	332	3,500 each
JAMAICA	**652**					
S Rose	88	75	72	75	310	
C Bernard	86	79	89	88	342	3,500 each
ISRAEL	**682**					
R Assyag	80	82	82	84	328	
J Avnaim	94	85	88	87	354	3,500 each

LEADING INDIVIDUAL SCORES

B Langer	69	68	66	69	272	$75,000
F Couples	66	71	70	68	275	50,000
E Els	69	71	72	66	278	35,000
N Price	70	69	71	68	278	35,000
J Van de Velde	66	70	71	72	279	20,000
R Allenby	72	68	70	70	280	15,000
S Torrance	68	69	71	73	281	
D Love III	71	69	71	70	281	
A Forsbrand	71	69	74	68	282	
M A Jimenez	72	70	72	68	282	
C Rocca	71	75	67	70	283	
M McNulty	71	68	72	72	283	
F Nobilo	74	69	69	71	283	
R Rafferty	71	69	73	71	284	
C Montgomerie	75	70	69	70	284	
D Barr	74	70	70	71	285	
J Rivero	73	72	66	74	285	
G Turner	73	73	64	75	285	
M Mouland	68	70	75	73	286	
D Gilford	69	73	72	72	286	
R Davis	70	70	72	74	286	
A Barcellos	76	70	70	71	287	
P R Martinez	74	73	69	71	287	
E Romero	71	70	72	75	288	
M James	76	74	68	70	288	

Price and McNulty reflect on what might have been; Zimbabwe finished second to America

5

Global Golf

EUROPE

UNITED STATES

AUSTRALASIA

JAPAN

REST OF THE WORLD

EUROPE

1993 PGA European Tour Review

Montgomerie climbs to the summit of a game without frontiers

José-Maria Olazabal and Nick Faldo at the finish of a memorable Irish Open

The photograph on this page may not be among the most visually striking in this book but it surely encapsulates much of what is presently so good about golf in Europe: a great English golfer commiserates with and is congratulated by a great Spanish golfer at the conclusion of a truly thrilling championship in Ireland.

The Irish Open at Mount Juliet saw one of the most exciting finishes of the season – Faldo produced a closing course record 65 to catch Olazabal, then beat him in a play-off – but the nature of the result was far from unusual. The following demonstrates just how international golf has become in Europe.

In 1993 a New Zealand player won the Italian Open, an Italian won in Paris and a Frenchman won in Rome; a Welsh golfer won the English Open, English golfers won in Portugal, Morocco and Switzerland and the Scottish Open was won by a Swede. It goes without saying that the German Open was won by a German, but a Scotsman won the Dutch Open, an Irishman the Austrian Open and a South African won in Jersey; as for the British Open at St George's, the famous Claret Jug went to an Australian who plays most of his golf in America.

Returning to the use of our picture, it does give one rather misleading impression, namely that Faldo and Olazabal enjoyed successful seasons in 1993. In fact, measured by their exalted standards, last year was a disappointing one for both players.

The win at Mount Juliet (his third successive Irish title) was Faldo's only win in Europe, although earlier in the year he did win another 'European' Tour event, the Johnnie Walker Classic in Singapore. He lost his Order of Merit title to Colin Montgomerie in the final event of the season; he was defeated in the final of the World Matchplay Championship at Wentworth and, despite making a marvellous defence, lost his Open Championship trophy to Greg Norman.

Olazabal fared far worse. He didn't win any tournaments at all in 1993 and slipped to 18th on the money list. While Faldo at least retained his number one Sony Ranking position, 'Ollie' plummeted from 4th place at the beginning of January to 15th by the end of December. And this was the player whom many people thought would dominate golf in the 1990s.

Nineteen ninety three, then, was Montgomerie's year in Europe. His rise to the top has been, if not meteoric, certainly swift. Since turning professional in 1987 the Scottish golfer has finished 52nd, 25th, 14th, 4th, 3rd and 1st in the Order of Merit. He will readily acknowledge that he was a trifle fortunate to leap-frog Faldo and claim the number one spot at Valderrama, for although his great friend (and now rival) played in the Volvo Masters, he was hampered by a wrist injury. But Montgomerie, the winner in July of the Heineken Dutch Open (see page 109), definitely finished the year in the style of a true champion. He described his final round at Valderrama in November as the finest of his life: to be able to overtake Faldo he needed nothing less than a win – and that is precisely what he achieved, scoring a 68 on the Sunday and setting a new record four round total for the tournament.

Italian Costantino Rocca was rarely out of the news in 1993

Alongside Montgomerie, the Italian Costantino Rocca is a worthy candidate for 'European Player of the Year', and yet he will probably look back on 1993 with slightly mixed feelings. Metaphorically speaking, one could suggest that he took himself (and the cause of Italian golf) about five steps forward and one step backwards. Two tour victories (the first of his career), sixth position on the money list and a Ryder Cup place (Italy's first) were tremendous achievements. Sadly, life is such that he will probably be remembered most in 1993 for the 'horrible little putt' that

Tour winners in 1993: Steven Richardson, Rodger Davis and Peter Baker

he missed at The Belfry.

Just as Rocca became the first Italian to play in the Ryder Cup, 24 year-old Joakim Haeggman became the first Swedish player to do so. After a brilliant year in 1992, Anders Forsbrand had been expected to claim that honour but he, it seems, is as inconsistent as Haeggman is consistent. A debut victory in the Spanish Open and 12 top ten finishes were proof of the young Swede's enormous potential.

It may not be too long either before a French player gets selected for Ryder Cup duty: Jean Van de Velde won the Roma Masters in April – the first Tour victory by a French player in 23 years – and his form subsequently would indicate that France may have unearthed, at long last, a major star.

Included in a shortlist of names to watch for in the future must also be that of Northern Ireland's Darren Clarke. He won the Alfred Dunhill Open in October at Royal Zoute in Belgium after courageously fending off the challenges of Faldo, Langer and Ballesteros, amongst others.

The young player who made the most dramatic impact of all in 1993 was undoubtedly England's Peter Baker. Regarded as a 'boy wonder' when he defeated Nick Faldo in a play-off to win the 1988 Benson and Hedges tournament he had since practically vanished without trace. One week at Woburn in June last year changed all that. Baker won the Dunhill British Masters by seven shots; in his second round he equalled the course record with a 64 and then, in an incredible final round, returned a 63. Pressure? He obviously thrives on it. Baker played the eleven holes between the 4th and the 14th in nine under par on Sunday. Two months later the 25 year-old had added the Scandinavian Masters title to his trophy cabinet after beating home favourite Anders Forsbrand in a sudden death play-off. Then, of course, there was his memorable performance at The Belfry.

The only player to win three times in

Europe last year was Sam Torrance, his victories coming in the Kronenbourg Open, Honda Open and the Heineken Open Catalonia. Mark James and David Gilford managed to win two events before the middle of March and Ian Woosnam came good late in the season (before he travelled to Sun City, that is); Bernhard Langer, on the other hand, was impressive throughout the year. There are some players who would happily rest on their laurels after a four shot victory in the Masters at Augusta but Langer is not one of them. In May he won the Volvo PGA Championship at Wentworth by six strokes and in August, won his fifth German Open title by five.

If the sheer audacity of Baker's win at Woburn made it the most impressive of 1993, Jesper Parnevik's victory in the Bell's Scottish Open at Gleneagles and Gordon Brand Jnr's in the European Open at East Sussex National

Bernhard Langer

American Fred Couples excelled at St Andrews in October

might be considered to be of equal quality. Both players led their respective events from start to finish and both so out-classed the rest of the field that they strolled home on the final day, winning at the proverbial canter.

Towards the end of the European season American golfers underlined their Ryder Cup supremacy by defeating England in the final of the Alfred Dunhill Cup at St Andrews. Fred Couples was easily the star performer of their side that week. (In November, Couples also guided America to an unprecedented treble, when he and Davis Love successfully defended the Heineken World Cup at Lake Nona.)

We cannot end without a word on Seve. What adjective does one use to sum up his year in 1993? A Spanish expletive probably. He finished in 42nd place in the Order of Merit and, for the first time since 1975, failed to win a European tournament. But anyone who writes Seve off does so at his peril. Not too long ago people were saying that Greg Norman was finished. At the age of 38 Norman returned last year to produce his greatest ever performance when it mattered most. Seve is 36.

The Seve we all know and love: Ballesteros had little to celebrate in 1993... but he'll be back

THE 1993 HEINEKEN DUTCH OPEN

Wayward Americans: John Daly (left) and Lee Janzen (below) missed a few fairways at Noordwijkse last July

A quick story: two Americans are on a golfing vacation in Scotland. They are playing one of the famous old links courses – let's say, Troon – and it is blowing a gale. They are struggling with the elements but trying desperately to keep their heads down. One of them slashes at his tee shot and, suspecting the worst, cries out 'Where on Earth did that go, did you see it?' His caddie interjects, 'I'm afraid you've hit a Clark Gable'. The two Americans look at each other incredulously, 'What in heaven's name does that mean?' And the caddie replies, 'Gone with the wind, sir'.

John Daly, winner of the 1991 USPGA Championship, and Lee Janzen, the newly crowned US Open champion came to Noordwijkse in Holland last July determined to win one of the premier events on the European circuit. Noordwijkse is a splendid links course – perhaps the finest on the continent – and after a fairly calm opening day

the wind picked up and began to blow fiercely... you can guess the rest.

As always, a very strong international field had been assembled for the 1993 Heineken Dutch Open. In addition to the US Open champion, the reigning US Masters champion was present – but then Germany's Bernhard

Wales v Scotland in Holland; Ian Woosnam and Colin Montgomerie in action at Noordwijkse

Langer was defending his title – so too were the Fijian Vijay Singh and South Africa's two leading players, David Frost and Ernie Els. Also in the starting line up were the rising stars of Australasian golf, Robert Allenby and Michael Campbell, while Ian Woosnam, José–Maria Olazabal, Sam Torrance, Anders Forsbrand, Peter Baker and Costantino Rocca were just some of the European stars on show… and, of course, there was Colin Montgomerie. Cometh links golf, cometh the wind, and cometh the wind, cometh 'Monty'.

The golf course and the elements were made for Montgomerie, a native of Troon, Scotland. It was 'Monty', remember, who stormed around a windswept Pebble Beach (America's greatest 'links' course) in the final round of the 1992 US Open. The big Scot finished third in that event, his valiant effort only failing to bring a famous victory because he left himself too much to do on Sunday. It was almost a similar story at Noordwijkse.

He was three shots behind surprise first round leader, David Russell, whose adventurous 65 included a three-off-the-tee at the 2nd, an eagle at the 11th and a chip-in birdie at the 18th, and after a 73 was four behind Ronan Rafferty (67-70) at the half-way stage.

On Saturday Argentina's Jose Coceres overtook the Irishman and, despite taking six at the par four 16th, Woosnam moved into the frame with a three under par 69 to add to opening rounds of 71-70. Montgomerie had a steady 71 but with a round to play was two behind Woosnam, three behind Rafferty and four strokes back of Coceres, who led with a total of 208. As for Langer, the sore neck that had been troubling him for some time was never likely to fare well in the conditions and the American, Australian and South African challengers were simply blown off course.

The weather on Sunday comprised a mixture of sun, rain and wind; there was even a 30 minutes stoppage for thunder and lightening. It was very tough for the players and only two managed to break 70 all day. One of these was the Frenchman, Jean Van de Velde, who earlier in the season had won the Roma Masters. Six behind Coceres at the start of play, he scored five birdies in the first 11 holes and at one point looked as if he might 'steal' the championship. Woosnam also looked a possible winner until he ran into trouble towards the end of his round; 'Woosie' returned a 73, Coceres a 74 and Rafferty had a disappointing 75. Van de Velde dropped a stroke at the very difficult 16th but his round of 68 eventually tied him with Coceres, one ahead of Woosnam. But there was one other player who broke 70 on stormy Sunday and that was 'Monty'. Perhaps the two key moments in his battling final round 69 were the 35 foot eagle putt he sank at the 11th and the par he salvaged at the 16th.

This year's British Open is at Turnberry, a course not unlike Noordwijkse, and situated just down the road from Troon. If the wind really blows... you'll know who to watch for.

22nd - 25th July

HEINEKEN DUTCH OPEN

NOORDWIJKSE

Colin Montgomerie	68	73	71	69	281	£108330
Jose Coceres	69	70	69	74	282	56450
Jean Van de Velde	73	70	71	68	282	56450
Ian Woosnam	71	70	69	73	283	32500
Ronan Rafferty	67	70	72	75	284	27530
Mark Roe	70	71	74	70	285	21125
Steen Tinning	71	70	69	75	285	21125
Paul Eales	68	74	74	70	286	16250
Olle Karlsson	76	71	69	71	287	12662
Jesper Parnevik	71	71	70	75	287	12662
Eamonn Darcy	70	74	69	74	287	12662
Jorge Berendt	68	73	73	73	287	12662
Tony Johnstone	75	69	73	71	288	10460
Marc Farry	71	74	72	72	289	9162
Paul McGinley	74	73	70	72	289	9162
Vijay Singh	72	70	73	74	289	9162
Anders Sorensen	70	69	73	77	289	9162
Sam Torrance	72	69	72	76	289	9162
David A Russell	65	75	72	78	290	7222
Philip Walton	72	72	74	72	290	7222
Per-Ulrik Johansson	70	75	69	76	290	7222
Lee Janzen	68	72	74	76	290	7222

'Monty' follows Bernhard Langer as the Heineken Dutch Open champion

1993 PGA European Tour Results

14th - 17th January
MADEIRA ISLAND OPEN
CAMPO DE GOLFE DA MADEIRA

Mark James	71	69	70	71	281	£41660
Paul Broadhurst	72	71	70	71	284	21710
Gordon J Brand	71	72	70	71	284	21710
Ronan Rafferty	73	73	67	72	285	11550
Jamie Spence	72	69	73	71	285	11550
Gordon Brand Jnr	69	75	72	70	286	7500
Glenn Ralph	72	74	69	71	286	7500
David Gilford	73	73	70	70	286	7500

28th - 31st January
DUBAI DESERT CLASSIC
EMIRATES GOLF CLUB, DUBAI

Wayne Westner	69	66	69	70	274	£66660
Retief Goosen	70	66	72	68	276	44440
Seve Ballesteros	71	68	69	69	277	22520
Barry Lane	70	69	68	70	277	22520
Paul McGinley	65	70	70	73	278	14313
Mark Davis	72	65	70	71	278	14313
Anders Forsbrand	73	66	68	71	278	14313
Ernie Els	71	72	67	71	281	10000

4th - 7th February
JOHNNIE WALKER CLASSIC
SINGAPORE ISLAND COUNTRY CLUB

Nick Faldo	67	68	66	68	269	£91660
Colin Montgomerie	68	67	69	66	270	61100
Choi Sang-Ho	69	67	71	67	274	34430
Greg Norman	71	68	68	68	275	25400
Steven Richardson	70	70	66	69	275	25400
Boonchu Ruangkit	67	72	68	69	276	19250
Fred Couples	73	65	70	69	277	15125
Frankie Minoza	70	69	71	67	277	15125

11th - 14th February
TURESPANA IBERIA-OPEN DE CANARIAS
GOLF DEL SUR, TENERIFE

Mark James	71	69	69	66	275	£58330
De Wet Basson	71	70	72	68	281	38880
Eamonn Darcy	69	76	65	74	284	21910
Eduardo Romero	72	73	71	69	285	14860
Andrew Murray	74	71	68	72	285	14860
Stephen Ames	77	74	67	67	285	14860
Wayne Riley	74	72	73	67	286	10500
David A Russell	73	74	72	68	287	8285

Mark James enjoyed two early season victories

18th - 21st February

Moroccan Open

GOLF ROYAL DE AGADIR

David Gilford	68	70	70	71	279	£62500
Stephen Ames	70	72	66	72	280	32550
Jamie Spence	67	69	72	72	280	32550
Robert Karlsson	75	67	73	69	284	19000
Vicente Fernandez	77	67	70	72	286	16000
Wayne Westner	70	71	73	73	287	12000
Magnus Sunesson	75	72	69	71	287	12000
Carl Mason	76	69	71	72	288	8433
Tony Johnstone	78	71	72	67	288	8433
Frank Nobilo	73	74	69	72	288	8433

25th - 28th February

Turespana Masters-Open de Andalucia

NOVO SANCTI PETRI, CADIZ

Andrew Oldcorn	70	71	73	71	285	£58330
Eduardo Romero	68	72	75	71	286	38880
Steven Richardson	69	71	73	74	287	21910
De Wet Basson	75	71	73	72	291	16165
Ian Palmer	69	77	70	75	291	16165
Costantino Rocca	77	69	75	71	292	11375
Wayne Westner	71	73	75	73	292	11373
Des Smyth	67	79	73	74	293	7856
Joakim Haeggman	69	72	77	75	293	7856
José-Maria Olazabal	71	71	75	76	293	7856

4th - 7th March

Turespana Open Mediterrania

EL SALER, VALENCIA

Frank Nobilo	71	69	67	72	279	£66660
David Feherty	70	69	72	69	280	34740
Gordon Brand Jnr	70	72	70	68	280	34740
Santiago Luna	67	72	72	70	281	15735
José-Maria Olazabal	71	69	75	66	281	15735
Thomas Levet	71	70	69	71	281	15735
Costantino Rocca	70	72	71	68	281	15735
Jim Payne	68	67	78	69	282	8232
Jesper Parnevik	71	67	73	71	282	8232
Mark Roe	69	70	70	73	282	8232
Mats Lanner	73	69	69	71	282	8232

11th - 14th March

Turespana Iberia-Open de Baleares

GOLF SANTA PONCA, MALLORCA

*Jim Payne	73	66	71	67	277	£50000
Anders Gillner	71	69	67	70	277	33330
David R Jones	76	68	70	64	278	18780
Andrew Sherborne	72	70	66	71	279	15000
Greg Turner	70	70	73	67	280	11600
Steen Tinning	69	69	70	72	280	11600
Ronan Rafferty	70	70	70	71	281	9000
Joakim Haeggman	72	67	73	70	282	6730
Derrick Cooper	70	72	70	70	282	6730
Ian Palmer	71	68	72	71	282	6730

18th - 21st March

Portuguese Open

VILA SOL GOLF CLUB, VILLAMOURA

*David Gilford	65	66	70	74	275	£41660
Jorge Berendt	63	71	69	72	275	27770
Frank Nobilo	66	68	72	71	277	12916
Gordon J Brand	68	72	70	67	277	12916
Mark James	69	73	66	69	277	12916
Martin Poxon	66	70	74	68	278	8750
Ricky Willison	68	69	71	72	280	6450
Fredrik Lindgren	74	66	69	71	280	6450
Sam Torrance	70	72	70	68	280	6450

25th - 28th March

Kronenbourg Open

GARDAGOLF CC, ITALY

Sam Torrance	69	68	73	74	284	£33330
Mike Miller	74	71	71	69	285	22220
Costantino Rocca	69	70	74	73	286	12520
Antoine Lebouc	73	76	71	68	288	7294
Brian Marchbank	72	72	74	70	288	7294
Paul McGinley	72	72	73	71	288	7294
Craig Cassells	71	69	75	73	288	7294
Stephen McAllister	70	73	71	74	288	7294
David Gilford	72	69	76	72	289	4460

* winner in play-off

15th - 18th April

ROMA MASTERS

CASTELGANDOLFO, ROME

*Jean Van de Velde	66	76	67	72	281	£50000
Greg Turner	72	68	70	71	281	33330
Costantino Rocca	68	68	74	72	282	18780
De Wet Basson	75	71	68	69	283	15000
Des Smyth	74	67	73	70	284	10733
Frank Nobilo	68	73	73	70	284	10733
Barry Lane	69	71	72	72	284	10733
David Gilford	73	73	70	69	285	7095
Gary Orr	73	72	68	72	285	7095

Jean Van de Velde becomes the first French golfer to win in Europe for 23 years

22nd - 24th April

HEINEKEN OPEN CATALONIA

OSONA MONTANYA GOLF CLUB, BRULL

Sam Torrance	71	63	67	201	£50000
Jay Townsend	66	69	69	204	33330
Andrew Sherborne	65	72	68	205	16890
Paul Way	66	73	66	205	16890
Jesper Parnevik	69	68	69	206	10733
Eamonn Darcy	69	68	69	206	10733
David Curry	69	73	64	206	10733
Gary Evans	68	69	70	207	6427
Ross Drummond	66	70	71	207	6427
Ian Woosnam	69	67	71	207	6427
José-Maria Olazabal	68	73	66	207	6427

28th April - 2nd May

AIR FRANCE CANNES OPEN

CANNES MOUGINS CC, ROUTE D'ANTIBES, MOUGINS

*Rodger Davis	68	64	69	70	271	£66660
Mark McNulty	69	70	68	64	271	44440
Pierre Fulke	66	66	72	68	272	22520
Jamie Spence	68	67	66	71	272	22520
Anders Forsbrand	68	68	68	69	273	16940
Jose Coceres	69	69	66	70	274	13000
Mike Harwood	69	71	68	66	274	13000
Carl Mason	68	70	68	69	275	8973
Barry Lane	68	68	68	71	275	8973
Brian Marchbank	66	70	71	68	275	8973

Sam Torrance savours a win in the Heineken Open Catalonia staged in the foothills of northern Spain

6th - 9th May

Benson and Hedges International Open

ST MELLION GOLF & COUNTRY CLUB, CORNWALL

Paul Broadhurst	69	69	67	71	276	£91660
José-Maria Olazabal	67	72	68	70	277	47765
Mark James	68	71	69	69	277	47765
Gordon Brand Jnr	67	69	71	72	279	25400
Joakim Haeggman	69	69	71	70	279	25400
Nick Faldo	70	70	74	67	281	19250
Roger Chapman	70	72	65	76	283	14176
Vijay Singh	68	75	70	70	283	14176
Colin Montgomerie	70	72	71	70	283	14176

The greatest golfing family in Germany pose for the cameras at Wentworth

13th - 16th May

Peugeot Open de Espana

REAL AUTOMOVIL CLUB DE ESPANA, MADRID

Joakim Haeggman	69	69	69	68	275	£83330
Ernie Els	70	68	69	70	277	43425
Nick Faldo	68	69	72	68	277	43425
José-Maria Olazabal	74	69	67	68	278	21233
Ian Woosnam	67	70	72	69	278	21233
Mats Lanner	72	64	73	69	278	21233
Justin Hobday	70	70	70	69	279	15000
Heinz P Thul	72	72	66	70	280	11216
Roger Chapman	70	72	71	67	280	11216
Peter Baker	70	69	70	71	280	11216

20th - 23rd May

Lancia Martini Italian Open

MODENA G&CC

Greg Turner	65	70	68	64	267	£73393
Jose Coceres	64	70	66	68	268	48898
Barry Lane	67	69	66	70	272	22760
Wayne Westner	66	72	69	65	272	22760
David Gilford	65	66	73	68	272	22760
Steven Richardson	65	69	70	69	273	15418
Ronan Rafferty	67	71	71	65	274	13215
Brian Marchbank	69	67	70	69	275	11013
Wayne Riley	72	70	66	68	276	9339
José-Maria Olazabal	68	70	69	69	276	9339

28th - 31st May

Volvo PGA Championship

WEST COURSE, WENTWORTH, SURREY

Bernhard Langer	70	69	67	68	274	£116660
Gordon Brand Jnr	69	71	73	67	280	52196
Frank Nobilo	72	67	70	71	280	52196
Colin Montgomerie	70	69	71	70	280	52196
Mark McNulty	72	71	69	69	281	29640
Tony Johnstone	74	66	69	74	283	24500
Glen Day	72	67	74	71	284	18036
Eduardo Romero	71	71	71	71	284	18036
Greg Turner	73	69	71	71	284	18036
Peter Mitchell	73	70	69	73	285	11865
Peter Fowler	73	71	71	70	285	11865
José-Maria Olazabal	74	70	73	68	285	11865

3rd - 6th June

Dunhill British Masters

WOBURN (DUKE'S COURSE), BUCKINGHAMSHIRE

Peter Baker	67	64	72	63	266	£100000
Carl Mason	68	67	69	69	273	66660
Tony Johnstone	70	70	68	66	274	37560
Ronan Rafferty	68	66	70	71	275	27700
Roger Chapman	70	69	69	67	275	27700
Joakim Haeggman	68	67	69	72	276	18000
David Feherty	66	68	72	70	276	18000
Jim Payne	68	70	68	70	276	18000
Glen Day	68	73	71	65	277	13440

10th - 13th June

HONDA OPEN

GUT KADEN, HAMBURG

*Sam Torrance	68	69	68	73	278	£83330
Ian Woosnam	67	72	68	71	278	37283
Johan Rystrom	69	66	71	72	278	37283
Paul Broadhurst	71	68	71	68	278	37283
Joakim Haeggman	71	71	71	66	279	19350
Bernhard Langer	69	68	72	70	279	19350
Mats Lanner	71	72	68	69	280	12883
Ian Palmer	67	72	72	69	280	12883
Jamie Spence	70	66	73	71	280	12883

17th - 20th June

JERSEY EUROPEAN AIRWAYS OPEN

LA MOYE, JERSEY

Ian Palmer	68	67	70	63	268	£50000
Sam Torrance	70	68	63	69	270	33330
Mark James	68	65	71	67	271	18780
Jim Payne	70	66	70	66	272	12733
Martin Gates	72	67	67	66	272	12733
Greg Turner	66	69	69	68	272	12733
Mark Roe	68	70	66	69	273	9000

24th - 27th June

PEUGEOT OPEN DE FRANCE

LE GOLF NATIONAL, PARIS

*Costantino Rocca	66	66	71	70	273	£83330
Paul McGinley	69	67	69	68	273	55550
Mark James	69	69	68	68	274	31300
Anders Forsbrand	68	71	69	67	275	23100
Mark Roe	67	71	68	66	276	13230
Jay Townsend	71	71	68	66	276	13230
Johan Rystrom	66	70	67	73	276	13230
Tony Johnstone	67	71	71	67	276	13230
David Feherty	67	70	70	69	276	13230
Jean Van de Velde	67	64	73	72	276	13230

*winner in play-off

1st - 4th July

CARROLLS IRISH OPEN

MOUNT JULIET GC, THOMASTOWN, CO KILKENNY

*Nick Faldo	72	67	72	65	276	£96630
José-Maria Olazabal	69	67	71	69	276	64380
David Frost	74	69	68	68	279	36310
Steven Richardson	71	68	72	69	280	29000
Costantino Rocca	71	70	71	69	281	24590
Retief Goosen	69	72	75	66	282	18850
Olle Karlsson	71	67	72	72	282	18850
Per-Ulrik Johansson	69	68	72	74	283	13030
Joakim Haeggman	71	68	72	72	283	13030
Wayne Westner	73	69	73	68	283	13030
Ian Woosnam	71	72	72	69	284	10670

7th - 10th July

BELL'S SCOTTISH OPEN

GLENEAGLES HOTEL (KINGS COURSE)

Jesper Parnevik	64	66	70	71	271	£100000
Payne Stewart	71	69	67	69	276	66660
Gary Orr	70	72	72	64	278	33780
Jose Rivero	77	66	68	67	278	33780
Paul Way	69	74	70	66	279	23200
Sam Torrance	73	65	71	70	279	23200
Christy O'Connor Jnr	71	70	70	70	281	18000
Roger Chapman	69	71	73	69	282	12352
Mark Roe	73	72	68	69	282	12352
Gary Evans	69	68	73	72	282	12352
Robert Lee	67	71	73	71	282	12352
Sandy Lyle	73	67	69	73	282	12352

22nd - 25th July

HEINEKEN DUTCH OPEN

NOORDWIJKSE

see page 111

29th July - 1st August

SCANDINAVIAN MASTERS

FORSGARDENS GC, GOTHENBURG, SWEDEN

*Peter Baker	67	71	68	72	278	£108330
Anders Forsbrand	67	71	71	69	278	72210
Nick Faldo	69	72	71	68	280	40690

David Feherty	68	73	70	71	282	30015
Rodger Davis	72	71	70	69	282	30015
Stephen Ames	71	68	71	73	283	22750
Colin Montgomerie	68	72	71	73	284	17875
Robert Karlsson	72	69	70	73	284	17875
Costantino Rocca	72	73	70	70	285	12222
Frank Nobilo	69	72	73	71	285	12222
Paul Way	71	69	71	74	285	12222

5th - 8th August

BMW International Open

MUNCHEN NORD-EICHENRIED

Peter Fowler	67	69	68	63	267	£83330
Ian Woosnam	65	68	68	69	270	55550
Bernhard Langer	66	69	70	66	271	23750
Anders Forsbrand	71	67	68	65	271	23750
Gary Orr	67	69	66	69	271	23750
Peter Mitchell	69	66	69	67	271	23750
Joakim Haeggman	68	66	69	69	272	15000
Mark McNulty	66	70	69	68	273	12500
De Wet Basson	66	68	70	70	274	11150
Jesper Parnevik	68	72	67	68	275	9595
Juan Quiros	67	70	69	69	275	9595

Peter Fowler scores a final round 63 to win the BMW International Open

12th - 15th August

Hohe Brucke Austrian Open

COLONY CLUB GUTENHOF, HIMBERG

*Ronan Rafferty	65	69	72	68	274	£41660
Anders Sorensen	70	67	68	69	274	27770
Per-Ulrik Johansson	70	67	70	68	275	15650
Jamie Taylor	66	71	68	71	276	11550
Sven Struver	72	63	72	69	276	11550
Paul Mayo	68	70	67	73	278	8125
Greg Turner	68	67	71	72	278	8125

19th - 22nd August

Murphy's English Open

THE FOREST OF ARDEN HOTEL GOLF & CC, NR. COVENTRY

Ian Woosnam	71	67	65	66	269	£100000
Costantino Rocca	70	68	64	69	271	66660
José-Maria Canizares	66	71	66	69	272	37560
Darren Clarke	68	72	68	70	278	27700
Ronan Rafferty	73	68	69	68	278	27700
Mark Roe	69	73	67	70	279	16860
Brian Marchbank	70	69	74	66	279	16860
Per-Ulrik Johansson	68	73	69	68	279	16860
Peter Mitchell	70	72	69	68	279	16860
Retief Goosen	74	67	70	69	280	11106
Howard Clark	71	69	68	72	280	11106
Joakim Haeggman	70	69	68	73	280	11106

26th - 29th August

Volvo German Open

GOLF CLUB HUBBELRATH, DUSSELDORF

Bernhard Langer	65	68	70	66	269	£108330
Peter Baker	68	66	71	69	274	56450
Robert Allenby	71	70	65	68	274	56450
Colin Montgomerie	68	71	70	66	275	30015
Darren Clarke	69	70	71	65	275	30015
David Feherty	67	69	69	71	276	21125
Joakim Haeggman	69	67	72	68	276	21125
David Gilford	69	74	65	69	277	13930
Johan Rystrom	65	72	70	70	277	13930
Peter O'Malley	68	68	71	70	277	13930
Gary Orr	67	70	70	70	277	13930

2nd - 5th September

CANON EUROPEAN MASTERS

CRANS-SUR-SIERRE, SWITZERLAND

Barry Lane	69	67	64	70	270	£102960
Miguel Angel Jimenez	67	68	63	73	271	53640
Seve Ballesteros	71	66	68	66	271	53640
Per-Ulrik Johansson	71	64	68	69	272	30900
Howard Clark	67	70	66	70	273	26200
Darren Clarke	69	66	71	68	274	20085
Gary Orr	69	68	68	69	274	20085
Paul Curry	69	70	65	71	275	13883
Nick Faldo	65	70	69	71	275	13883
Colin Montgomerie	66	72	69	68	275	13883
Torsten Giedeon	68	69	69	70	276	10650
Robert Karlsson	72	68	69	67	276	10650
Anders Forsbrand	72	68	67	69	276	10650

9th - 12th September

GA EUROPEAN OPEN

EAST SUSSEX NATIONAL GC, UCKFIELD

Gordon Brand Jnr	65	68	71	71	275	£100000
Phillip Price	70	68	71	73	282	52110
Ronan Rafferty	69	73	68	72	282	52110
Olle Karlsson	68	73	67	75	283	27700
Frank Nobilo	73	69	69	72	283	27700
Ian Woosnam	70	75	69	70	284	19500
Paul Lawrie	72	70	69	73	284	19500
Steven Richardson	72	70	70	73	285	14220
Darren Clarke	74	72	65	74	285	14220
Sam Torrance	71	75	70	70	286	12000
Des Smyth	73	75	71	68	287	10660
Rodger Davis	72	77	69	69	287	10660

16th - 19th September

TROPHEE LANCOME

ST NOM LA BRETECHE, PARIS

Ian Woosnam	64	70	68	65	267	£91500
Sam Torrance	69	65	68	67	269	61000
David Feherty	69	63	69	69	270	28600
Barry Lane	71	66	66	67	270	28600
Mark James	65	66	72	67	270	28600
Nick Faldo	69	67	69	66	271	18000
Fred Couples	70	65	65	71	271	18000
Mark Roe	68	70	68	67	273	13750
Jose Rivero	70	66	66	72	274	12250

30th September - 3rd October

MERCEDES GERMAN MASTERS

MONSHEIM, STUTTGART

Steven Richardson	67	66	70	68	271	£100000
Robert Karlsson	68	69	70	66	273	66660
Chip Beck	72	63	69	70	274	37560
Jesper Parnevik	70	72	68	66	276	27700
Bernhard Langer	73	64	70	69	276	27700
José-Maria Olazabal	69	69	72	67	277	21000
David Frost	66	70	71	71	278	16500
Tom Watson	74	67	69	68	278	16500

7th - 10th October

ALFRED DUNHILL OPEN

ROYAL ZOUTE, KNOKKE-LE-ZOUTE, BELGIUM

Darren Clarke	68	68	66	68	270	£100000
Nick Faldo	68	68	69	67	272	52110
Vijay Singh	68	69	71	64	272	52110
Rodger Davis	74	67	64	68	273	23600
Bernhard Langer	72	64	72	65	273	23600
Seve Ballesteros	67	65	71	70	273	23600
Gordon Brand Jnr	66	71	68	68	273	23600

Darren Clarke is challenging Ronan Rafferty's position as Ireland's top golfer

14th - 17th October

ALFRED DUNHILL CUP

OLD COURSE, ST ANDREWS, FIFE

Round Robin Event

GROUP ONE	Matches Won	Games Won	Total Score	Prize Per Man
Ireland	2	7	659	—
Spain	2	5	661	£15000
Zimbabwe	2	4	664	8500
Argentina	0	2	672	6500
GROUP TWO	Matches Won	Games Won	Total Score	Prize Per Man
England	2	6	659	—
South Africa	2	5	647	£15000
Taiwan	1	4	691	8500
Mexico	1	3	691	6500
GROUP THREE	Matches Won	Games Won	Total Score	Prize Per Man
USA	3	8	653	—
Paraguay	2	5	668	£15000
Scotland	1	4	661	8500
Wales	0	1	679	6500
GROUP FOUR	Matches Won	Games Won	Total Score	Prize Per Man
Sweden	3	7	653	—
Canada	2	5	656	£15000
Japan	1	3	677	8500
Australia	0	3	680	6500

SEMI-FINALS

England bt Ireland 3-0

James (67) bt Rafferty (70) Baker (72) bt Feherty (73)

Faldo (70) bt McGinley (74)

USA bt Sweden 2-1

Stewart (68) lost to Parnevik (66)

Daly (68) bt Haeggman (71) Couples (67) bt Forsbrand (69)

Sweden and Ireland receive £31,666 per man

FINAL

USA bt England 2-1

Stewart (74) lost to James (70) Couples (68) bt Faldo (69)

Daly (70) bt Baker (73)

America receive £100,000 per man, England £50,000 per man

Leading individual scorer: Fred Couples (USA)

Des Smyth was a popular winner of the Madrid Open

28th - 31st October

MADRID OPEN

REAL CLUB DE LA PUERTA DE HIERRO

Des Smyth	65	68	68	71	272	£66660
Wayne Westner	70	65	68	72	275	26605
Jose Rivero	68	72	66	69	275	26605
Domingo Hospital	68	69	68	70	275	26605
Mark Roe	69	66	71	69	275	26605
David Feherty	68	72	70	66	276	11230
Santiago Luna	70	70	67	69	276	11230
Eduardo Romero	73	66	68	69	276	11230
David J Russell	74	67	68	67	276	11230

4th - 7th November

VOLVO MASTERS

VALDERRAMA, SOTOGRANDE, SPAIN

Colin Montgomerie	69	70	67	68	274	£125000
Darren Clarke	69	73	65	68	275	83400
David Gilford	68	72	67	69	276	46950
Vijay Singh	72	72	67	70	281	37500
Ian Woosnam	71	67	71	73	282	32100
Mark McNulty	73	73	67	71	284	26800
Carl Mason	76	70	72	67	285	23000
Jesper Parnevik	70	75	69	72	286	18250
Costantino Rocca	75	71	72	68	286	18250
Retief Goosen	72	75	71	69	287	13560
Rodger Davis	74	74	70	69	287	13560

1993 PGA European Tour Winners Summary

TOURNAMENT · WINNERS

January

MADEIRA ISLAND OPEN	Mark James	(Eng)
DUBAI DESERT CLASSIC	Wayne Westner	(SA)

February

JOHNNIE WALKER CLASSIC	Nick Faldo	(Eng)
TURESPANA IBERIA-OPEN DE CANARIAS	Mark James	(Eng)
MOROCCAN OPEN	David Gilford	(Eng)
TURESPANA MASTERS OPEN DE ANDALUCIA	Andrew Oldcorn	(Eng)

March

TURESPANA OPEN MEDITERRANIA	Frank Nobilo	(NZ)
TURESPANA IBERIA-OPEN DE BALEARES	Jim Payne	(Eng)
PORTUGUESE OPEN	David Gilford	(Eng)
KRONENBOURG OPEN	Sam Torrance	(Scot)

April

OPEN V33 DU GRAND LYON	Costantino Rocca	(It)
ROMA MASTERS	Jean Van de Velde	(Fr)
HEINEKEN OPEN CATALONIA	Sam Torrance	(Scot)
AIR FRANCE CANNES OPEN	Rodger Davis	(Aus)

May

BENSON AND HEDGES INTERNATIONAL OPEN	Paul Broadhurst	(Eng)
PEUGEOT OPEN DE ESPANA	Joakim Haeggman	(Swe)
LANCIA MARTINI ITALIAN OPEN	Greg Turner	(NZ)
VOLVO PGA CHAMPIONSHIP	Bernhard Langer	(Ger)

June

DUNHILL BRITISH MASTERS	Peter Baker	(Eng)
HONDA OPEN	Sam Torrance	(Scot)
JERSEY EUROPEAN AIRWAYS OPEN	Ian Palmer	(SA)
PEUGEOT OPEN DE FRANCE	Costantino Rocca	(It)

July

CARROLLS IRISH OPEN	Nick Faldo	(Eng)
BELL'S SCOTTISH OPEN	Jesper Parnevik	(Swe)
122ND OPEN CHAMPIONSHIP	Greg Norman	(Aus)
HEINEKEN DUTCH OPEN	Colin Montgomerie	(Scot)
SCANDINAVIAN MASTERS	Peter Baker	(Eng)

August

BMW INTERNATIONAL OPEN	Peter Fowler	(Aus)
HOHE BRUCKE AUSTRIAN OPEN	Ronan Rafferty	(N.Ire)
MURPHY'S ENGLISH OPEN	Ian Woosnam	(Wal)
VOLVO GERMAN OPEN	Bernhard Langer	(Ger)

September

CANON EUROPEAN MASTERS	Barry Lane	(Eng)
GA EUROPEAN OPEN	Gordon Brand Jnr	(Scot)
TROPHEE LANCOME	Ian Woosnam	(Wal)
MERCEDES GERMAN MASTERS	Steven Richardson	(Eng)

October

ALFRED DUNHILL OPEN	Darren Clarke	(N.Ire)
* ALFRED DUNHILL CUP	United States	
* TOYOTA WORLD MATCHPLAY CHAMPIONSHIP	Corey Pavin	(USA)
MADRID OPEN	Des Smyth	(Ire)

November

VOLVO MASTERS	Colin Montgomerie	(Scot)

* PGA European Tour Approved Special Event

1993 PGA European Tour

VOLVO ORDER OF MERIT: TOP 100

Europe's Number One

1	Colin Montgomerie	£613,682
2	Nick Faldo	558,738
3	Ian Woosnam	501,353
4	Bernhard Langer	469,569
5	Sam Torrance	421,328
6	Costantino Rocca	403,866
7	Peter Baker	387,988
8	Darren Clarke	369,675
9	Gordon Brand Jnr	367,589
10	Barry Lane	339,218
11	Mark James	335,589
12	Ronan Rafferty	311,125
13	Steven Richardson	304,015
14	Frank Nobilo	294,598
15	Joakim Haeggman	287,370
16	David Gilford	273,301
17	Jesper Parnevik	272,511
18	José-Maria Olazabal	249,493
19	Paul Broadhurst	243,588
20	Wayne Westner	226,297
21	Greg Turner	222,296
22	David Feherty	216,479
23	Anders Forsbrand	213,509
24	Mark Roe	199,994
25	Jean Van de Velde	199,437
26	Rodger Davis	198,180
27	Carl Mason	183,757
28	Eduardo Romero	175,430
29	Jose Coceres	174,679
30	Gary Orr	173,979
31	Peter Fowler	173,073
32	Des Smyth	169,729
33	De Wet Basson	163,858
34	Ernie Els	162,827
35	Miguel Angel Jimenez	162,572
36	Jim Payne	160,570
37	Jose Rivero	159,879
38	Paul McGinley	159,786
39	Vijay Singh	159,110
40	Mark McNulty	152,097
41	Tony Johnstone	151,223
42	Seve Ballesteros	148,854
43	Robert Karlsson	147,386
44	Retief Goosen	147,256
45	Ian Palmer	139,420
46	Per-Ulrik Johansson	136,592
47	Peter Mitchell	133,127
48	Roger Chapman	131,769
49	Stephen Ames	131,743
50	Jamie Spence	125,887
51	Howard Clark	120,086
52	Andrew Oldcorn	115,705
53	Brian Marchbank	113,888
54	Paul Way	113,148
55	Mats Lanner	106,765
56	Olle Karlsson	103,919
57	Paul Lawrie	95,067
58	Jay Townsend	90,012
59	Johan Rystrom	88,949
60	Phillip Price	86,901
61	Santiago Luna	86,333
62	Gordon J Brand	83,842
63	Steen Tinning	83,409
64	Andrew Sherborne	81,210
65	Glen Day	79,944
66	Gary Evans	79,809
67	Sandy Lyle	79,224
68	Sven Struver	79,133
69	Jorge Berendt	78,492
70	Robert Allenby	77,150
71	Anders Gillner	71,780
72	Domingo Hospital	67,577
73	Mark Davis	66,986
74	Anders Sorensen	66,081
75	Silvio Grappasonni	64,280
76	Magnus Sunesson	61,956
77	Peter O'Malley	61,039
78	José Maria Canizares	60,283
79	Russell Claydon	60,271
80	Paul Curry	59,900
81	John McHenry	58,799
82	Wayne Riley	57,786
83	Mike McLean	57,748
84	Andrew Murray	56,345
85	Paul Eales	55,425
86	Pierre Fulke	54,895
87	Derrick Cooper	54,320
88	Eamonn Darcy	53,865
89	Martin Gates	52,578
90	Richard Boxall	52,365
91	Vicente Fernandez	51,228
92	Philip Walton	49,902
93	Mark Mouland	48,340
94	Jeremy Robinson	48,223
95	Andre Bossert	47,994
96	Marc Farry	47,555
97	Adam Hunter	46,901
98	Ross Drummond	46,361
99	David Curry	46,211
100	David A Russell	45,627

The World Matchplay Championship

America rediscovers the art of matchplay

Corey Pavin lines up a putt at Wentworth during his semi-final match with Colin Montgomerie

Remember Bill Rogers – clean-cut, pencil slim and deadly accurate with his irons? He won an Open at Sandwich and in 1979 became the fifth and (until 1993) last American to win the World Matchplay title at Wentworth. The 13 championships in between were monopolised by European golfers and Australia's Greg Norman. An American player reached the final on only two occasions during those years: Ben Crenshaw in 1981 and Jeff Sluman in 1992. Seve Ballesteros won the event five times, Norman three times, Ian Woosnam twice, Nick Faldo twice and Sandy Lyle once. Like Europe's domination of the Masters at Augusta, it couldn't last forever.

The 12 players invited to the 1993 Toyota World Matchplay Championship represented no fewer than ten nations and once the first round ties had been played, the quarter-finals comprised eight players from eight different countries.

When John Daly and Corey Pavin were announced as the two US competitors not too many people rushed off to their bookmakers to place vast sums on an American success. Neither Daly nor Pavin had won an event on the US Tour in 1993 and, as it was the third week in October neither was likely to. Daly, it was agreed, would humiliate the par fives at Wentworth but would also spend too much of his time clambering amongst the bracken. By contrast, Pavin was thought to be too short off the tee; he would fight like a terrier – as he had done so effectively during the recent Ryder Cup at The Belfry – but with the famous West Course playing longer than usual after a damp summer, the lightweight 'Chaplinesque' figure, as Peter Alliss described him, would be at too great a disadvantage.

There were two other major obstacles to overcome. Firstly, the two Americans were not seeded, which meant that in order to win the championship they must play four 36 hole matches in four days and secondly, they must beat the likes of England's Nick Faldo (the defending champion), Germany's Bernhard Langer (the Masters champion), Zimbabwe's Nick Price (the 'hottest' player on the US Tour) and Wales' Ian Woosnam (an acknowledged Wentworth specialist), all of whom were seeded.

The pundits were right about John Daly. The first round pitted him and his Killer Whale driver against the Australian Open champion, Steve Elkington. He thrilled the crowds for 32 holes and he lost 5 & 4. Corey Pavin faced an intriguing contest with England's 'golden boy' Peter Baker; it was a re-match in a sense, for the two had been drawn against each other in the Ryder Cup singles. Baker got the better of the American on that occasion, and won memorably on the final green. But this time Pavin took his revenge and won 4 & 3. In the other first round ties, David Frost of South Africa crushed a very out-of-sorts Ballesteros by 7 & 6 and Scotland's Colin Montgomerie scraped home against the Japanese player Yoshinori Mizumaki at the 37th hole.

The second round results were a little more surprising. The four seeds entered the fray on Friday and three of them were promptly knocked out. The one exception was Nick Faldo who, though not playing at his imperious best, was good enough to end the challenge of Elkington, the conqueror of John Daly. The Masters champion (and winner of the PGA Championship at Wentworth in May) was comprehensively beaten 6 & 4 by Montgomerie. The Scot produced some fine golf, especially after lunch when he was five under par for the 14 holes played. Woosnam lost narrowly to David Frost (2 & 1) but the best golf of the quarter-final stage was played by Corey Pavin and Nick Price. Given the nature of matchplay, scoring is always approximate, but Price was reckoned to have gone round in 67 in the morning yet found himself 3 down at lunch. If anything, the quality of their golf was superior in the afternoon and when Price surrendered at the 17th Pavin was 10 under par for the day.

An October weekend at Wentworth: although in our dreams the West Course at such times is always basking in autumnal sunshine, the reality is often different: Indian Summers are rare in Surrey. This year it was thick woolly jumper-weather, or in Corey Pavin's case, woolly hat-weather. It was an interesting sight seeing him playing against Montgomerie in the semi-finals. It was the giant fluffy bear versus the garden gnome – the gnome that looked and walked like Charlie Chaplin. 'Monty's' problem, however (and it was to be Faldo's problem on Sunday) had little to do with the weather: Pavin was beginning to play like Bill Rogers. From tee to green he hit the ball with unerring accuracy and was equally deadly with his putter. Pavin's match with Montgomerie turned out to be easily the better of the two semi-finals. The American was 3 down after four holes, 3 up with four holes to play and all-square after 36. He eventually won at the first extra hole.

Given the almost wintry conditions and their personalities, it is unlikely that many words were exchanged between Faldo and Frost in the other semi-final. The defending champion gained a 2 & 1 victory, but again it seemed that he was either holding something in reserve, or his game was not quite 100%.

For the second year running Faldo towered over his Final opponent. In 1992 he did so in more than just the physical sense – but Pavin is a far better player than Jeff Sluman. As the world number one, Faldo was the favourite to win, of course, even if it was universally agreed that the American had played the better golf throughout the week. The two had played together in the final round of the Open at St George's in July and against one another (in foursomes) at the Ryder Cup in September and Faldo scored better on both occasions.

When he won the first hole of the afternoon round to go 2 up in the match, Faldo appeared to be in control of affairs. But Pavin, you will recall, can fight like a terrier and over the next ten holes he reeled off an extraordinary tally of seven birdies. From being 2 down he was suddenly 2 up with seven holes to play. Faldo responded like the true champion he is by eagling the 12th; but Pavin won the next and was still 2 up with three to play.

On a cold and blustery day it was strange being out of breath but the golf was that good. There was, however, still one final twist in the tale. Faldo won the 16th (or 34th) with a par and the 17th (35th) with a birdie to square the match. What more – Faldo to eagle the last for an amazing victory? How about Pavin to win it with a tame par five!

Faldo (left) comes to grief at the final hole. (Below) Pavin is on his way to a famous victory

1993 Toyota World Matchplay Championship

October 21 - 24, Wentworth (West Course), Surrey

FIRST ROUND
Steve Elkington (Aus) beat John Daly (USA) 5 & 4
David Frost (SA) beat Seve Ballesteros (Sp) 7 & 6
Corey Pavin (USA) beat Peter Baker (Eng) 4 & 3
Colin Montgomerie (Scot) beat Yoshinori Mizumaki (Jap) at 37th
First round losers received £25,000

SECOND ROUND
Nick Faldo (Eng) beat Steve Elkington 4 & 3
David Frost beat Ian Woosnam (Wal) 2 & 1
Corey Pavin beat Nick Price (Zim) 2 & 1
Colin Montgomerie beat Bernhard Langer (Ger) 6 & 4
Second round losers received £35,000

SEMI-FINALS
Nick Faldo beat David Frost 2 & 1
Corey Pavin beat Colin Montgomerie at 37th

PLAY-OFF FOR THIRD & FOURTH PLACES
David Frost beat Colin Montgomerie 2 & 1
Frost received £60,000; Montgomerie £50,000

FINAL
Corey Pavin beat Nick Faldo 1 hole
Pavin received £160,000; Faldo £90,000

Corey Pavin, America's first World Matchplay champion since 1979

The World Matchplay

ROLL · OF · HONOUR

Year	Winner	Year	Winner	Year	Winner
1964	Arnold Palmer	1974	Hale Irwin	1984	Seve Ballesteros
1965	Gary Player	1975	Hale Irwin	1985	Seve Ballesteros
1966	Gary Player	1976	David Graham	1986	Greg Norman
1967	Arnold Palmer	1977	Graham Marsh	1987	Ian Woosnam
1968	Gary Player	1978	Isao Aoki	1988	Sandy Lyle
1969	Bob Charles	1979	Bill Rogers	1989	Nick Faldo
1970	Jack Nicklaus	1980	Greg Norman	1990	Ian Woosnam
1971	Gary Player	1981	Seve Ballesteros	1991	Seve Ballesteros
1972	Tom Weiskopf	1982	Seve Ballesteros	1992	Nick Faldo
1973	Gary Player	1983	Greg Norman	1993	Corey Pavin

1993 WPG European Tour Review

Spirit of the Solheim Cup spills over

We could commence this tale in the company of lush bougainvillea at the Kelab Rahmen Putra Golf Club near Kuala Lumpur and finish by basking on the French Rivera at St Maxime. That is where the WPG European Tour began and ended its tournament schedule in 1993. But even if we were to relate fastidiously the details of who won what and where in between, it would still only provide half the picture. This is because to follow the fortunes of women golfers from the 'Old World' it is necessary to keep one eye on events in the 'New World'.

Inspired by their brilliant victory in the 1992 Solheim Cup (and notwithstanding

Sweden's latest rookie sensation: Annika Sorenstam drives at Woburn during the Ford Classic

administrative upheavals beyond the scope of this review) Europe's women achieved unprecedented success on last year's LPGA Tour in America. Several of the players from that winning team must have spent a small fortune on air travel in 1993 for they seemed to be constantly jetting to and fro across the Atlantic. Perhaps what made last year such an interesting one in Europe was the fact that even when the transatlantic stars appeared en masse they didn't always dominate. Indeed, on a number of occasions they were outplayed, if not by emerging Europeans then by a handful of determined golfers from Australia.

At one instant we were cheering 'Alfie the Great' as Sweden's Helen Alfredsson captured the LPGA's first major championship of the year, and the next we were heralding 'Annika the Great', as her fellow Swede, Annika Sorenstam started to piece together a remarkable rookie season in Europe.

There were 11 events on the WPG European Tour in 1993 (at least 18 are planned for this year) and although Sorenstam failed to win any of them she probably made a bigger impact than anybody else. She played in nine tournaments and finished second on four occasions, including on her European debut in the Ford Classic. Three times she missed out on a play-off by a stroke and only once failed to finish in the top 12. She ended the year in third place on the Money List and led the 1994 Solheim Cup Standings (making an automatic selection to the European team to play at The Greenbrier in October very likely).

Unfortunately for the 23 year-old Swedish golfer the one event in which she played poorly was the Weetabix Women's British Open, the richest and most prestigious tournament in Europe. By contrast, Australian Karen Lunn chose that week to play the best golf of her life.

It was mid August and Patty Sheehan was back at Woburn to defend her title; so too was America's rising star, Brandie Burton (who a fortnight later would win the final LPGA Major of the year) and of course all of Europe's leading players.

Karen Lunn wins the Weetabix British Open

Although it was an exciting week – two holes-in-one on the first day, record crowds, blue skies and an incredible final round 64 from American Jane Geddes that included 10 birdies and an eagle – Lunn turned the championship into a one-woman exhibition. She won by eight shots with rounds of 71-69-

68-67; Burton finished second and Scotland's Kathryn Marshall was a distant third, 11 shots behind the winner. And this was the same Karen Lunn who had been so frustrated with her game 12 months earlier that she had contemplated giving it up altogether!

The Woburn victory was Lunn's second of 1993 for it was she who triumphed amid the lush bougainvillea in Malaysia. The event was the KRP World Ladies' Classic and the Australian won after a play-off with the Tour's 1992 Rookie of the Year, Sandrine Mendiburu. She also headed the Order of Merit at the end of the season, with winnings of £81,266. Not to be totally overshadowed, her sister, Mardi Lunn also claimed a European Tour title last year when she won the European Ladies' Classic in Germany and Corinne Dibnah raised the Australian flag in Holland with a win in the Holiday Inn Leiden Open.

French heroine, Marie-Laure de Lorenzi

So, 1993 was a great year for Swedish and Australian golfers – but it was also a vintage one for the British. The country's top two players, Laura Davies and Trish Johnson both enjoyed hugely successful seasons in America. Davies won the important McDonald's Championship in May while Johnson recorded stunning back-to-back victories in April. In Europe it was Davies who was definitely the more successful. She came second to Lunn in the Order of Merit and was involved in the two best finishes of the year – one she won and one she lost.

The Hennessy Ladies' Cup always seems to produce a thrilling final day's play and 1993 saw a titanic battle between two former US Open champions when Lotte Neumann defeated Davies in a play-off with a birdie at the first extra hole. At Tytherington in the Waterford Dairies English Open Davies just managed to get the better of Marie-Laure de Lorenzi to retain her title after the two had pulled almost ten strokes clear of the field on the final day.

As there were additional victories for Davies in Thailand at the beginning of the year, and in Australia in December, it meant that she gained wins in four different continents during 1993 – something no other golfer (male or female) was able to achieve last year.

Lora Fairclough and Helen Dobson are two more British golfers who will have special memories of 1993. Both secured maiden Tour victories: Fairclough won the IBM Open in Stockholm by five shots – quite a feat given the strength of the Swedish contingent she had to beat, and Dobson overcame the entire Solheim Cup winning side to snatch the BMW European Masters crown at Bercuit in Belgium.

Seven days after that victory, Dobson finished just a stroke behind Davies and Neumann in the Hennessy Cup after producing a closing round of 66, the highlight of which was a hole-in-one at the 8th. She seemed to go from strength-to-strength and at the beginning of September in America Dobson defeated Dottie Mochrie in a play-off to win her first LPGA title. Mochrie had been the number one golfer in the world in 1992 whilst Dobson finished a modest 36th in the European Order of Merit.

The Ford Classic was mentioned briefly above (Sorenstam finishing second on her European debut); for the second year running it was won by an Italian golfer, with Federica Dassu following Stefania Croce's very popular win in 1992. Neither Dassu nor Croce could win the Italian Ladies' Open, the penultimate event on the 1993 Tour, but then perhaps only Karen Lunn in her best British Open form could have prevented Spain's 23 year-old Amaya Arruti from winning that week. 'Amazing Amaya', the headlines repeated for four days in succession as she led the tournament from start to finish, shooting scores of 67-65-68-70. The most 'amazing' aspect of her victory came with the realisation that the Italian Open was only her sixth professional appearance.

The 'best of British': transatlantic stars Laura Davies (left) and Trish Johnson

A much more experienced winner emerged in the final WPG European Tour event of 1993, although that player hadn't actually won a tournament for three years. A more popular or more appropriate triumph it is difficult to imagine: France's Marie-Laure de Lorenzi was back on the winners' rostrum – and at the French Open of all places.

Perfect timing means everything in golf.

THE 1993 WEETABIX WOMEN'S BRITISH OPEN

12 - 15 August, Woburn G & CC

LEADING · SCORES

K Lunn	71	69	68	67	275	£50,000
B Burton	75	70	68	70	283	32,000
K Marshall	73	71	69	73	286	21,000
L Wen-Lin	70	71	74	72	287	14,350
J Geddes	76	75	72	64	287	14,350
P Sheehan	75	70	72	72	289	10,500
L Davies	69	76	75	70	290	7,300
M L de Lorenzi	73	77	72	68	290	7,300
S Strudwick	72	71	73	74	290	7,300
C Nilsmark	76	71	74	69	290	7,300
A Nicholas	74	73	70	74	291	5,400
T Johnson	72	75	77	69	293	5,400
D Reid	76	75	74	68	293	4,670
C Hjalmarsson	77	74	68	74	293	4,670
H Alfredsson	77	71	74	71	293	4,670
S Gronberg Whitmore	76	70	79	69	294	4,180
K Orum	75	72	73	74	294	4,180
S Gautrey	76	75	69	74	294	4,180
C Duffy	75	76	71	73	295	3,880
R Hast	77	71	72	75	295	3,880
J Soulsby	76	75	73	72	296	3,685
C Figg-Currier	75	75	72	74	296	3,685
G Stewart	74	75	76	72	297	3,505
P Meunier	73	76	77	71	297	Am
J Morley	77	74	74	72	297	Am
V Michaud	79	73	70	75	297	3,505
T Abitbol	77	74	74	73	298	3,145
F Dassu	70	75	75	78	298	3,145
X Wunsch-Ruiz	73	79	71	75	298	3,145
D Hanna	74	73	73	78	298	3,145

Former British Open champions, Laura Davies and Corinne Dibnah couldn't prevent Karen Lunn from claiming a runaway victory at Woburn

1993 WPG European Tour Summary

TOURNAMENT · WINNERS

KRP World Ladies' Classic	Karen Lunn	(Aus)
Ford Golf Classic	Federica Dassu	(It)
Holiday Inn Leiden Open	Corinne Dibnah	(Aus)
BMW European Masters	Helen Dobson	(GB)
Hennessy Ladies' Cup	Liselotte Neumann	(Swe)
The European Ladies' Classic	Mardi Lunn	(Aus)
Weetabix Women's British Open	Karen Lunn	(Aus)
IBM Ladies' Open	Lora Fairclough	(GB)
Ladies' English Open	Laura Davies	(GB)
Italian Ladies' Open	Amaya Arruti	(Sp)
Var French Open	Marie-Laure de Lorenzi	(Fr)

Sweden's Lotte Neumann, winner of the Hennesey Ladies' Cup

LEADING · MONEY · WINNERS

1	Karen Lunn	£81,266
2	Laura Davies	64,938
3	Annika Sorenstam	55,927
4	Marie-Laure de Lorenzi	46,479
5	Liselotte Neumann	39,530
6	Helen Dobson	38,179
7	Corinne Dibnah	34,429
8	Lora Fairclough	28,625
9	Federica Dassu	27,707
10	Dale Reid	25,553
11	Mardi Lunn	23,495
12	Laurette Maritz-Atkins	23,145
13	Alison Nicholas	22,772
14	Catrin Nilsmark	21,052
15	Carin Hjalmarsson	19,309
16	Amaya Arruti	18,579
17	Trish Johnson	17,452
18	Janet Soulsby	16,393
19	Karina Orum	15,841
20	Mette Hageman	15,664
21	Susan Moon	14,450
22	Gillian Stewart	14,431
23	Kristal Parker	13,735
24	Regine Lautens	13,682
25	Helen Wadsworth	13,567
26	Debbie Petrizzi	13,365
27	Helen Alfredsson	13,116
28	Lisa Hackney	12,656
29	Shani Waugh	12581
30	Karine Espinasse	11,565
31	Sofia Gronberg Whitmore	11,348
32	Debbie Dowling	11,295
33	Corinne Soules	10,689
34	Valerie Michaud	10,365
35	Julie Forbes	9,605
36	Claire Duffy	9,235
37	Veronique Palli	9,197
38	Allison Shapcott	8,856
39	Sarah Gautrey	8,799
40	Sally Prosser	8,281
41	Caroline Hall	7,674
42	Catherine Panton-Lewis	7,590
43	Jane Hill	7,325
44	Xonia Wunsch-Ruiz	6,925
45	Diane Barnard	6,455
46	Susan Shapcott	6,139
47	Karen Pearce	5,990
48	Rae Hast	5,723
49	Asa Gottmo	5,606
50	Anne Jones	5,521

United States

1993 US PGA Tour Review

After a year of Love and Couples, Americans were forced to pay the Price

'Player of the Year' Nick Price

It wasn't Nicklaus-style domination by any stretch of the imagination but, by and large, Nick Price was the man to beat in 1993, just as Fred Couples and Davis Love (numbers one and two on the 1992 US Money List) had been in the previous season.

Price was the leading moneywinner, with winnings of almost $1.5million and received both the Vardon Trophy for maintaining the lowest stroke average (69.11) and the PGA Player of the Year Award.

He won four events on the PGA Tour last year, which was one victory more than Paul Azinger achieved. His greatest triumph in 1993 occurred in March at the Players Championship, golf's so-called fifth Major. He won that event in brilliant fashion, compiling rounds of 64-68-71-67 to win by five shots from Bernhard Langer, and we all know the kind of form Langer was in last Spring. The other three victories all came during the summer, Price scoring a spectacular hatrick in the three events he entered during a five week period. He won the Canon Greater Hartford Open with a final round of 65, the Western Open – sponsored rather appropriately in the circumstances by Sprint – with rounds of 64-71-67-67 for a second five stroke victory, this time over Greg Norman and, returning to the Tour after a two week break in Europe, captured the Federal Express St Jude Classic by three shots, scoring 69-65-66-66.

It was an odd year for America and its leading golfers. In various team events around the world the USA proved to be nigh-on invincible but at home, on the PGA Tour, American golfers regularly finished second. Not only was the famous Augusta Green Jacket won by a European (for the seventh time in 11 years) but an inordinate amount of silverware was appropriated by players from the Southern Hemisphere.

Lee Janzen, winner of the Phoenix Open in February and the US Open in June

Zimbabwean Nick Price was, of course, the principal beneficiary but there were several others and if Greg Norman had taken advantage of a few more of the opportunities he created it could have verged on the embarrassing. Greg's sole US victory came in March in the Doral Ryder Open but he very nearly won the USPGA Championship and he should have won the year-ending Tour Championship. His fellow Australian and a Tour rookie, Brett Ogle won the AT & T National Pro-Am at Pebble Beach, one of the Tour's most sought-after titles. Grant Waite of New Zealand and Fijian Vijay Singh also claimed debut victories in America. South African players were particularly impressive in 1993 with both David Frost and Fulton Allem winning twice. Frost entered a Price-like vein of form in September when, in successive weeks, he won the Canadian Open at Glen Abbey and the Hardee's Classic at Coal Valley. Allem was an unexpected winner of the prestigious Colonial and World Series tournaments.

Paying the Price? At times it seemed more like rape and pillage. Thank heavens, then, for the US Open. And thank heavens for Lee Janzen, Payne Stewart and Paul Azinger.

The US Open is more than just America's most important championship, it is also the one that foreigners hardly ever seem to win. Janzen, Stewart and Azinger finished 1-2-3 in 1993 and, in terms of the season as a whole, they were America's three most successful players. In addition to winning the US Open, Janzen won the Phoenix Open in February. Stewart, whom Janzen defeated in a head-to-head tussle at Baltusrol, failed to win on the PGA Tour but came second on no fewer than four occasions. Stewart played equally well overseas: he finished runner-up in the Scottish Open at Gleneagles, shot a closing 63 at St George's in the British Open and won a tournament in Morocco. He also pocketed an obscene amount of money in November, the result of winning the Skins Game for the third year running.

Azinger, however, was clearly America's best golfer in 1993. Victory in the PGA Championship at Inverness – his first major title – was obviously the highlight of his year but he was also the central figure in the year's most exciting finish. It happened in the Memorial Tournament at Muirfield Village where, with one hole to play, he trailed his playing partner Payne Stewart by one stroke.

John Cook plays from a fairway bunker during the Masters at Augusta; 1993 was a disappointing year for Cook

Tom Kite, pictured during his amazing week at the Bob Hope Chrysler Classic

Australia's Brett Ogle captured the AT&T National Pro-Am at Pebble Beach

Both hit their approach shots into a fairly cavernous greenside trap then, moments after Stewart had played a fine recovery to within six feet or so of the pin, Azinger holed out à la Bob Tway at Inverness in 1986. (An omen for what was to happen at the USPGA Championship in August if ever there was one). Stewart then missed his par putt to tie – as well as the putt that followed!

Price and Azinger were the only players to collect more than two titles but in addition to the doubles of Frost, Allem and Janzen, five other players achieved two PGA Tour victories in 1993.

Davis Love won the first event of the year, the Tournament of Champions and also the season's penultimate event in Las Vegas. Love won the latter in October by the year's biggest winning margin, a massive eight strokes. In between times, however, he didn't play nearly as well as he had in 1992. The same comment most definitely applies to John Cook, a three-time winner in 1992 but who fell from third place on the Money List to a relatively lowly 45th in 1993.

Jim Gallagher Jnr, Larry Mize, Phil Mickelson and Tom Kite were the other players to win on more than one occasion. For Mickelson it meant his first two professional victories (he also won on the Tour while still an amateur) in a career that promises great things – greatness even.

Tom Kite winning twice is hardly major news, although the manner of his first victory in the Bob Hope Chrysler Classic certainly was, for in winning by six shots he established a new Tour record of 35 under par. It was a five-day event, but still, scores of 67-67-65-64-62 are rather difficult to comprehend.

On reflection, Kite's 'demolition job' in the Californian desert is a candidate for 'performance of the year'. Either of Price's wins in the Players Championship and Western Open must also have strong claims. The most stunning win though, was probably that of Fulton Allem at Firestone in the World Series, where he stormed through the field on the final day to win with a round of 62.

Greg Norman also had a 62 last year, in addition to numerous scores around the 64 to 66 mark; in fact, Norman's scoring average in America was better than that of Nick Price – an amazing 68.90; unfortunately an insufficient number of tournament rounds made him ineligible for the Vardon Trophy. Norman's 62 came during the second round of the Doral Ryder Open in Miami.

To suggest that 1993 was a mixed year for Norman would be an understatement. In

(Above) Fulton Allem won two tournaments on the US Tour in 1993. (Below) Fred Couples

world terms, because of his British Open victory, glory certainly outweighed tragedy but when considering his American adventures in isolation, it is debatable. The way he lost to Azinger in the PGA Championship play-off was pretty desperate; mercifully it happened after the win at Royal St George's. In the final event of the US season, the Tour Championship at the Olympic Club in San Francisco, Norman led Jim Gallagher by two strokes with nine holes to play; at stake was more than just the huge $540,000 first prize, for he still had a chance of becoming Leading Moneywinner, ahead of Price. Somehow – and only he knows how – he managed to bogey four of the last seven holes to lose by one shot. For those of us watching, the Great White Shark may sometimes be a danger to our blood pressures but the world of golf would be immeasurably poorer without him.

Greg Norman 'presented' the end-of-season Tour Championship prize to Jim Gallagher (above)

1993 US PGA Tour Results

January 7 - 10

Infiniti Tournament of Champions

LA COSTA CC, CARLSBAD, CA

D Love III	67	67	69	69	272	$144000
T Kite	69	71	69	64	273	86400
P Azinger	65	69	70	71	275	46400
M O'Meara	70	70	68	67	275	46400
J Cook	73	68	68	69	278	31000
B Faxon	71	69	67	71	278	31000
D Forsman	68	71	69	71	279	27225
S Pate	73	66	71	69	279	27225
J Huston	70	73	68	70	281	24825
M Calcavecchia	68	72	70	72	282	23025
F Couples	70	70	72	70	282	23025

January 14 - 17

United Airlines Hawaiian Open

WAIALAE CC, HONOLULU, HI

H Twitty	63	68	70	68	269	$216000
J Sindelar	71	68	66	68	273	129600
P Azinger	67	68	69	70	274	81600
K Clearwater	72	66	68	71	277	49600
J Maggert	68	71	68	70	277	49600
B Ogle	67	70	70	70	277	49600
N Henke	69	71	71	67	278	38700
D Love III	69	68	71	70	278	38700

January 21 - 24

Northern Telecom Open

TUCSON NATIONAL, TUCSON, AZ

L Mize	68	66	70	67	271	$198000
J Maggert	70	66	70	67	273	118800
M Allen	68	70	68	68	274	52800
R Freeman	71	68	69	66	274	52800
J Gallagher Jr	75	66	67	66	274	52800
D Hart	66	66	69	73	274	52800
B Andrade	63	73	69	70	275	36850
L Clements	69	67	70	70	276	29700
R Gamez	69	67	72	68	276	29700
R Maltbie	70	68	70	68	276	29700
P Mickelson	67	65	69	75	276	29700
C Parry	67	72	72	65	276	29700

January 28 - 31

Phoenix Open

TPC OF SCOTTSDALE, PHOENIX, AZ

L Janzen	67	65	73	68	273	$180000
A Magee	69	70	64	72	275	108000
M Allen	66	70	70	70	276	48000
M Springer	70	69	68	69	276	48000
K Triplett	69	67	69	71	276	48000
R Wrenn	66	68	68	74	276	48000
K Clearwater	68	72	71	66	277	32250
M Wiebe	67	70	70	70	277	32250
T Lehman	69	66	73	70	278	28000
G Morgan	71	65	74	68	278	28000

February 4 - 7

AT & T Pebble Beach National Pro-Am

THREE COURSES AT PEBBLE BEACH, CA

B Ogle	68	68	69	71	276	$225000
B Brown	70	68	69	72	279	135000
T Dodds	70	68	70	72	280	65000
J Sindelar	69	72	70	69	280	65000
G Twiggs	69	72	70	69	280	65000
L Janzen	71	67	72	71	281	45000
C Beck	72	71	69	70	282	40312
G Waite	71	70	72	69	282	40312

February 10 - 14

Bob Hope Chrysler Classic

FOUR COURSES AT PALM SPRINGS, CA

T Kite	67	67	64	65	62	325	$198000
R Fehr	66	66	70	62	67	331	118800
S Simpson	71	69	66	63	66	335	74800
K Clearwater	68	66	68	70	64	336	43312
J Gallagher Jr	69	68	67	69	63	336	43312
J Haas	66	66	71	65	68	336	43312
B Lohr	68	66	66	66	70	336	43312

B Glasson	70	64	66	67	70	337	34100
F Couples	68	64	68	66	72	338	29700
S Elkington	69	63	66	68	72	338	29700
W Levi	68	66	66	69	69	338	29700

February 18 - 21

BUICK INVITATIONAL OF CALIFORNIA

TORREY PINES GC, SAN DIEGO, CA

P Mickelson	75	69	69	65	278	$180000
D Rummells	77	64	71	70	281	108000
P Stewart	72	66	75	70	283	68000
J Don Blake	73	75	70	67	285	41333
J Haas	70	72	71	72	285	41333
G Twiggs	73	73	69	70	285	41333
K Clearwater	75	72	70	69	286	32250
J Sindelar	77	68	70	71	286	32250

February 25 - 28

NISSAN LOS ANGELES OPEN

RIVIERA CC, PACIFIC PALISADES, CA

T Kite	73	66	67	206	$180000
D Barr	71	72	66	209	66000
F Couples	71	67	71	209	66000
D Hammond	69	69	71	209	66000
P Stewart	72	66	71	209	66000
P Azinger	72	68	70	210	28187
J Don Blake	67	72	71	210	28187
R Fehr	72	67	71	210	28187
P Jacobsen	73	68	69	210	28187
J Maggert	71	73	66	210	28187
J Mudd	71	68	71	210	28187
G Twiggs	72	67	71	210	28187
H Twitty	70	72	68	210	28187

March 4 - 7

DORAL RYDER OPEN

DORAL CC, MIAMI, FL

G Norman	65	68	62	70	265	$252000
P Azinger	67	66	68	68	269	123200
M McCumber	69	67	66	67	269	123200
D Frost	70	64	68	68	270	67200
S Lyle	69	67	68	68	272	56000
F Couples	68	67	71	67	273	48650
N Faldo	72	65	70	66	273	48650
T Kite	66	73	69	67	275	43400
S Hoch	71	67	69	69	276	40600
C Beck	70	72	72	63	277	31033
L Janzen	71	71	70	65	277	31033
J Adams	72	67	70	68	277	31033
S Elkington	68	72	67	70	277	31033
E Humenik	67	71	69	70	277	31033
J Nicklaus	69	68	67	73	277	31033

Left-hander Phil Mickelson won twice on the PGA Tour in 1993

March 11 - 14

HONDA CLASSIC

WESTON HILLS CC, FT LAUDERDALE, FL

* F Couples	64	73	70	207	$198000
R Gamez	68	71	68	207	118800
L Mize	69	67	72	208	74800
D Mast	68	69	72	209	52800
C Parry	67	71	72	210	44000
E Dougherty	70	74	67	211	32135
M Smith	69	72	70	211	32135
F Zoeller	66	75	70	211	32135
D Frost	68	69	74	211	32135
J McGovern	71	69	71	211	32135

* winner in play-off

March 18 - 21
THE NESTLE INVITATIONAL
BAY HILL CLUB & LODGE, ORLANDO, FL

B Crenshaw	71	70	69	70	280	$180000
R Mediate	72	72	70	68	282	74666
V Singh	70	72	71	69	282	74666
D Love III	71	69	71	71	282	74666
E Humenik	73	69	72	70	284	40000
B Langer	71	70	71	73	285	33500
M McCumber	72	71	71	71	285	33500
M O'Meara	71	72	72	70	285	33500
J Sindelar	72	70	73	71	286	29000

March 25 - 28
THE PLAYERS CHAMPIONSHIP
TPC AT SAWGRASS, PONTE VEDRA, FL

N Price	64	68	71	67	270	$450000
B Langer	65	69	70	71	275	270000
G Morgan	68	71	72	65	276	145000
G Norman	66	70	68	72	276	145000
M O'Meara	67	71	66	73	277	100000
P Azinger	68	69	68	73	278	80937
K Green	70	67	69	72	278	80937
R Mediate	68	71	68	71	278	80937
N Ozaki	72	68	68	70	278	80937
T Watson	70	72	69	68	279	67500
J Edwards	66	69	72	73	280	53000
D Forsman	71	67	73	69	280	53000
M Hulbert	71	67	72	70	280	53000

April 1 - 4
FREEPORT-MCMORAN CLASSIC
ENGLISH TURN G & CC, NEW ORLEANS, LA

M Standly	71	71	72	67	281	$180000
R Cochran	75	68	70	69	282	88000
P Stewart	70	70	73	69	282	88000
G Norman	77	69	70	68	284	48000
V Singh	72	73	72	68	285	40000
S Hoch	72	74	72	69	287	32375
G Kraft	72	71	69	75	287	32375
N Lancaster	72	73	71	71	287	32375
D Mast	76	72	70	69	287	32375

April 8 - 11
THE MASTERS
AUGUSTA NATIONAL, AUGUSTA, GA

See p.33

April 8 - 11
DEPOSIT GUARANTY CLASSIC
HATTIESBURG CC, HATTIESBURG, MS

G Kraft	65	70	64	68	267	$54000
M Hatalsky	69	65	68	66	268	26400
T Rhyan	66	70	64	68	268	26400
B Jaeckel	68	65	66	70	269	11310
M Kuramoto	69	68	66	66	269	11310
D Martin	70	66	68	65	269	11310
L Mattiace	65	70	67	67	269	11310
G Waite	72	65	69	63	269	11310

April 15 - 18
MCI HERITAGE CLASSIC
HARBOUR TOWN GL, HILTON HEAD, SC

D Edwards	68	66	70	69	273	$202500
D Frost	67	67	70	71	275	121500
P Azinger	70	68	66	73	277	50737
I Baker-Finch	68	70	69	70	277	50737
M McCumber	68	68	70	71	277	50737
D Pooley	67	70	70	70	277	50737
F Zoeller	70	69	68	70	277	50737
J Cook	69	67	69	73	278	31500
T Lehman	70	70	70	68	278	31500
G Morgan	71	72	69	66	278	31500
S Pate	71	67	68	72	278	31500

April 22- 25
K-MART GREATER GREENSBORO OPEN
FOREST OAKS CC, GREENSBORO, NC

* R Mediate	74	67	71	69	281	$270000
S Elkington	71	68	69	73	281	162000
P Azinger	73	67	70	72	282	78000
D Hart	72	65	74	71	282	78000
G Morgan	71	69	69	73	282	78000
D Edwards	70	71	70	72	283	50250
L Janzen	71	71	70	71	283	50250

April 29 - May 2

SHELL HOUSTON OPEN

TPC AT THE WOODLANDS, TX

* J McGovern	67	64	68	199	$234000
J Huston	65	66	68	199	140400
D Hammond	67	65	68	200	67600
B McCallister	64	65	71	200	67600
P Stewart	66	68	66	200	67600
L Mize	68	64	69	201	46800
F Allem	66	70	67	203	39162
S Elkington	70	65	68	203	39162
L Roberts	67	67	69	203	39162

May 6 - 9

BELLSOUTH CLASSIC

ATLANTA CC, MARIETTA, GA

N Henke	67	69	68	67	271	$216000
M Calcavecchia	67	67	67	72	273	89600
N Price	69	67	64	73	273	89600
T Sieckmann	70	64	70	69	273	89600
F Allem	73	68	67	66	274	48000
M Springer	69	66	68	72	275	43200
B Andrade	67	66	73	70	276	33700
B Claar	70	68	67	71	276	33700
J Johnston	71	67	64	74	276	33700
L Mize	69	69	68	70	276	33700

May 13 - 16

GTE BYRON NELSON CLASSIC

TPC AT LAS COLINAS, IRVING, TX

S Simpson	65	66	68	71	270	$216000
B Mayfair	71	61	69	70	271	89600
C Pavin	69	68	67	67	271	89600
DA Weibring	68	65	69	69	271	89600
F Couples	71	63	70	68	272	43800
D Frost	68	66	69	69	272	43800
P Stewart	70	66	68	68	272	43800
M Calcavecchia	67	65	74	67	273	34800
R Floyd	66	69	70	68	273	34800
L Rinker	68	69	67	69	273	34800

May 20 - 23

KEMPER OPEN

TPC AT AVENEL, POTOMAC, MD

G Waite	66	67	72	70	275	$234000
T Kite	70	65	69	72	276	140400
M Bradley	69	71	69	68	277	75400
S Hoch	70	69	70	68	277	75400
B Estes	68	70	74	66	278	52000
J Anderson	68	73	68	70	279	46800
B Mayfair	70	69	72	69	280	40516
C Parry	71	69	71	69	280	40516
L Janzen	71	67	70	72	280	40516

New Zealander Grant Waite wins the Kemper Open

May 27 - 30

Southwestern Bell Colonial

COLONIAL CC, FORT WORTH, TX

F Allem	66	63	68	67	264	$234000
G Norman	69	64	64	68	265	140400
J Maggert	65	68	68	66	267	88400
L Roberts	66	70	66	66	268	57200
D Waldorf	65	69	69	65	268	57200
D Edwards	69	67	63	70	269	43550
J Huston	66	70	66	67	269	43550
T Watson	69	64	71	65	269	43550
K Clearwater	71	61	69	69	270	36400
C Pavin	70	65	67	68	270	36400

June 3 - 6

Memorial Tournament

MUIRFIELD VILLAGE GC, DUBLIN, OH

P Azinger	68	69	68	69	274	$252000
C Pavin	69	70	69	67	275	151200
P Stewart	69	66	67	74	276	95200
F Couples	67	68	73	69	277	50750
B Faxon	69	69	70	69	277	50750
J Haas	67	70	72	68	277	50750
J McGovern	67	71	69	70	277	50750
G Norman	68	68	74	67	277	50750
M Ozaki	67	70	73	67	277	50750
B Glasson	69	69	68	72	278	36400
D Love III	66	72	69	71	278	36400

June 10 - 13

Buick Classic

WESTCHESTER CC, RYE, NY

* V Singh	72	68	74	66	280	$180000
M Wiebe	72	75	67	66	280	108000
D Frost	70	72	73	66	281	58000
L Janzen	69	72	68	72	281	58000
T Lehman	74	69	70	69	282	38000
M Smith	72	73	69	68	282	38000
C Beck	71	72	74	66	283	31166
P Stewart	74	72	68	69	283	31166
B Gilder	72	72	69	70	283	31166

June 17 - 20

US Open

BALTUSROL, SPRINGFIELD, NJ

See p.45

June 24 - 27

Canon Greater Hartford Open

TPC AT RIVER HIGHLANDS, CROMWELL, CT

N Price	67	70	69	65	271	$180000
D Forsman	66	69	72	65	272	88000
R Maltbie	65	71	71	65	272	88000
C Pavin	67	65	73	69	274	48000
K Perry	68	69	70	68	275	38000
M Springer	69	65	73	68	275	38000
J Cook	73	68	71	65	277	30125
B Kamm	69	75	69	64	277	30125
R Mediate	68	70	72	67	277	30125
D Pooley	70	70	66	71	277	30125

1993 saw Fiji's Vijay Singh capture his first US tournament

July 1 - 4

SPRINT WESTERN OPEN

COG HILL CC, LEMONT, IL

N Price	64	71	67	67	269	$216000
G Norman	69	68	67	70	274	129600
B Lohr	72	69	67	69	277	81600
J Adams	72	71	63	72	278	49600
B Henninger	71	73	66	68	278	49600
M Wiebe	65	73	71	69	278	49600
M Allen	71	68	70	70	279	33700
R Fehr	71	68	71	69	279	33700
D Forsman	67	73	69	70	279	33700
P H Horgan III	69	74	68	68	279	33700
C Strange	69	68	69	73	279	33700
D Tewell	70	69	68	72	279	33700

July 8 - 11

ANHEUSER-BUSCH CLASSIC

KINGSMILL GC, WILLIAMSBURG, VA

J Gallagher Jr	66	68	70	65	269	$198000
C Beck	68	68	67	68	271	118800
D Rummells	67	71	66	68	272	57200
C Strange	67	69	68	68	272	57200
L Wadkins	67	71	64	70	272	57200
J Hallet	70	70	68	65	273	38225
L Roberts	70	68	69	66	273	38225

July 22 - 25

NEW ENGLAND CLASSIC

PLEASANT VALLEY CC, SUTTON, MA

P Azinger	67	69	64	68	268	$180000
J Delsing	73	67	65	67	272	88000
B Fleisher	70	67	66	69	272	88000
B Clampett	.63	71	67	73	274	44000
J Sindelar	68	67	70	69	274	44000
B Bryant	70	65	70	70	275	32375
P Jacobsen	68	71	68	68	275	32375
C Strange	70	70	65	70	275	32375
W Wood	68	65	70	72	275	32375

July 29 - August 1

FEDERAL EXPRESS ST JUDE CLASSIC

TPC AT SOUTHWIND, MEMPHIS, TN

N Price	69	65	66	66	266	$198000
R Fehr	68	66	68	67	269	96800
J Maggert	67	65	71	66	269	96800
F Zoeller	67	68	65	70	270	52800
G Morgan	69	69	64	69	271	44000
F Funk	68	69	65	70	272	38225
T Kite	70	67	69	66	272	38225
J Delsing	72	69	71	61	273	33000
C Strange	71	66	69	67	273	33000

August 5 - 8

BUICK OPEN

WARWICK HILLS G & CC, GRAND BLANC, MI

L Mize	64	69	71	68	272	$180000
F Zoeller	69	65	66	73	273	108000
G Norman	68	73	68	65	274	68000
J Don Blake	69	71	67	69	276	44000
C Pavin	71	65	71	69	276	44000
S Elkington	67	72	70	68	277	33500
F Funk	68	71	67	71	277	33500
S Lamontagne	67	70	70	70	277	33500

August 12 - 15

PGA CHAMPIONSHIP

INVERNESS, TOLEDO, OH

See p.71

August 19 - 22

THE INTERNATIONAL

CASTLE PINES GC, CASTLE ROCK, CO

P Mickelson	45	$234000
M Calcavecchia	37	140400
P Blackmar	33	88400
G Norman	31	57200
S Simpson	31	57200
B Faxon	28	45175
S Pate	28	45175
S Kendall	26	40300

The 1993 Canadian Open champion: South African David Frost achieved a one shot win over Fred Couples at Glen Abbey

August 26 - 29

NEC World Series of Golf

FIRESTONE CC, AKRON, OH

F Allem	68	68	72	62	270	$360000
C Stadler	71	69	68	67	275	149333
J Gallagher Jr	66	75	66	68	275	149333
N Price	69	67	71	68	275	149333
V Singh	73	70	68	66	277	80000
D Edwards	66	69	72	72	279	72000
S Elkington	69	67	72	72	280	62366
D Frost	68	69	71	72	280	62366
G Norman	69	69	69	73	280	62366
G Waite	72	70	75	65	282	54100

September 2 - 5

Greater Milwaukee Open

TUCKAWAY CC, FRANKLIN, WI

* B Mayfair	67	66	69	68	270	$180000
M Calcavecchia	72	64	67	67	270	88000
T Schulz	69	67	68	66	270	88000
B Lietzke	69	66	69	67	271	44000
R Zokol	67	68	68	68	271	44000
K Green	69	66	69	68	272	36000
D Hammond	69	65	70	69	273	33500

* winner in play-off

September 9 - 12

Canadian Open

GLEN ABBEY GC, OAKVILLE, ONTARIO

D Frost	72	70	69	68	279	$180000
F Couples	70	71	70	69	280	108000
B Bryant	68	70	70	74	282	68000
C Stadler	71	73	71	69	284	41333
B Lietzke	71	72	71	70	284	41333
S Stricker	66	69	74	75	284	41333
B Glasson	70	73	71	71	285	33500
P Blackmar	69	71	72	74	286	30000
D Hart	69	71	74	72	286	30000
B Chamblee	70	70	76	71	287	22166
J Gallagher Jr	73	74	68	72	287	22166
P H Horgan III	72	73	72	70	287	22166
N Price	68	74	71	74	287	22166
E Dougherty	71	70	70	76	287	22166

September 16 - 19

Hardee's Classic

OAKWOOD, COAL VALLEY, IL

D Frost	68	63	64	64	259	$180000
P Stewart	66	68	67	65	266	88000
D A Weibring	66	65	66	69	266	88000
B Tway	69	67	67	65	268	48000
J Huston	70	68	66	65	269	36500
D Ogrin	66	70	68	65	269	36500
M Schuchart	69	65	69	66	269	36500

September 23 - 26

BC Open

EN-JOIE GC, ENDICOTT, NY

B McAllister	68	71	65	67	271	$144000
D Watson	69	70	68	65	272	86400
B Glasson	66	72	68	67	273	54400
G Kraft	70	70	68	67	275	33066
M Lye	67	71	69	68	275	33066
D Ogrin	71	71	64	69	275	33066
D Mast	68	72	71	65	276	26800

September 30 - October 3

Buick Southern Open

CALLAWAY GARDENS, PINE MOUNTAINS, GA

* J Inman	71	73	64	70	278	$126000
B Andrade	68	70	73	67	278	46200
M Brooks	72	70	72	64	278	46200
B Bryant	69	72	70	67	278	46200
B Estes	70	69	67	72	278	46200
R Cochran	74	71	65	69	279	24325
T Lehman	70	65	76	68	279	24325

October 7 - 10

Walt Disney World/Oldsmobile Classic

THREE COURSES AT LAKE BUENA VISTA, FL

J Maggert	66	65	66	68	265	$198000
G Kraft	69	69	64	66	268	118800
K Green	70	68	63	69	270	52800
L Roberts	66	68	67	69	270	52800
C Stadler	68	67	68	67	270	52800
T Tryba	64	68	67	71	270	52800

October 14 - 17

H-E-B Texas Open

OAK HILLS CC, SAN ANTONIO, TX

* J Haas	68	65	66	64	263	$180000
B Lohr	68	64	67	64	263	108000
B Andrade	66	66	69	66	267	68000
B Estes	66	71	64	67	268	48000
M Dawson	69	67	65	68	269	32750
D Edwards	68	66	66	69	269	32750
D Forsman	64	68	67	70	269	32750
T Lehman	71	63	65	70	269	32750
G Morgan	66	66	70	67	269	32750
M Standly	66	71	65	67	269	32750

October 20 - 24

Las Vegas Invitational

THREE COURSES AT LAS VEGAS, NV

D Love III	67	66	67	65	66	331	$252000
C Stadler	67	66	69	72	65	339	151200
P Azinger	66	67	72	68	67	340	72800
D Edwards	72	66	68	67	67	340	72800
B Estes	68	68	68	67	69	340	72800
J Huston	69	66	69	71	67	342	46900
B Tway	71	68	68	67	68	342	46900
R Zokol	68	67	68	69	70	342	46900
G Morgan	64	68	72	70	69	343	40600

October 28 -31

Tour Championship

OLYMPIC CLUB, SAN FRANCISCO, CA

J Gallagher Jr	63	73	72	69	277	$540000
D Frost	68	68	69	73	278	198750
J Huston	72	68	68	70	278	198750
G Norman	72	67	68	71	278	198750
S Simpson	68	70	70	70	278	198750
R Fehr	69	69	70	71	279	108000
M Calcavecchia	69	69	75	67	280	96000
T Kite	69	68	72	71	280	96000
C Pavin	68	73	72	67	280	96000
F Couples	74	72	70	65	281	83100

November 4 - 7

Kapalua International

KAPALUA, MAUI, HI

F Couples	69	68	67	70	274	$180000
B McCallister	74	66	70	68	278	104000
D Love III	70	72	69	68	279	65000
P Jacobsen	67	74	67	73	281	42500
N Henke	69	73	67	73	282	34000
D Peoples	73	65	69	75	283	34000

Davis Love stormed to victory in Las Vegas

1993 US PGA TOUR

TOURNAMENT · WINNERS

January

Tournament	Winner	
INFINITI TOURNAMENT OF CHAMPIONS	Davis Love III	(US)
HAWAIIAN OPEN	Howard Twitty	(US)
NORTHERN TELECOM OPEN	Larry Mize	(US)
PHOENIX OPEN	Lee Janzen	(US)

February

Tournament	Winner	
AT & T NATIONAL PRO-AM	Brett Ogle	(Aus)
BOB HOPE CHRYSLER CLASSIC	Tom Kite	(US)
BUICK INVITATIONAL	Phil Mickelson	(US)
NISSAN LOS ANGELES OPEN	Tom Kite	(US)

March

Tournament	Winner	
DORAL RYDER OPEN	Greg Norman	(Aus)
HONDA CLASSIC	Fred Couples*	(US)
NESTLE INVITATIONAL	Ben Crenshaw	(US)
THE PLAYERS CHAMPIONSHIP	Nick Price	(Zim)

April

Tournament	Winner	
FREEPORT McMORAN CLASSIC	Mike Standly	(US)
THE MASTERS	Bernhard Langer	(Ger)
DEPOSIT GUARANTY CLASSIC	Greg Kraft	(US)
MCI HERITAGE CLASSIC	David Edwards	(US)
K MART GR. GREENSBORO OPEN	Rocco Mediate*	(US)
SHELL HOUSTON OPEN	Jim McGovern*	(US)

May

Tournament	Winner	
BELLSOUTH CLASSIC	Nolan Henke	(US)
GTE BYRON NELSON CLASSIC	Scott Simpson	(US)
KEMPER OPEN	Grant Waite	(NZ)
SOUTHWESTERN BELL COLONIAL	Fulton Allem	(SA)

June

Tournament	Winner	
THE MEMORIAL	Paul Azinger	(US)
BUICK CLASSIC	Vijay Singh*	(Fij)
UNITED STATES OPEN	Lee Janzen	(US)
CANON GREATER HARTFORD OPEN	Nick Price	(Zim)

July

Tournament	Winner	
CENTEL WESTERN OPEN	Nick Price	(Zim)
ANHEUSER-BUSCH CLASSIC	Jim Gallagher Jnr	(US)
NEW ENGLAND CLASSIC	Paul Azinger	(US)
FED EX ST JUDE CLASSIC	Nick Price	(Zim)

August

Tournament	Winner	
BUICK OPEN	Larry Mize	(US)
PGA CHAMPIONSHIP	Paul Azinger	(US)
THE INTERNATIONAL	Phil Mickelson	(US)
NEC WORLD SERIES OF GOLF	Fulton Allem	(SA)

September

Tournament	Winner	
GREATER MILWAUKEE OPEN	Billy Mayfair*	(US)
CANADIAN OPEN	David Frost	(SA)
HARDEE'S GOLF CLASSIC	David Frost	(SA)
BC OPEN	Blaine McAllister	(US)
BUICK SOUTHERN OPEN	John Inman*	(US)

October

Tournament	Winner	
WALT DISNEY/OLDSMOBILE CLASSIC	Jeff Maggert	(US)
HEB TEXAS OPEN	Jay Haas*	(US)
LAS VEGAS INVITATIONAL	Davis Love III	(US)
TOUR CHAMPIONSHIP	Jim Gallagher Jr	(US)

November

Tournament	Winner	
KAPALUA INTERNATIONAL	Fred Couples	(US)

* Winner in play-off

1993 US PGA TOUR

LEADING MONEY WINNERS

America's Number One

1	Nick Price	$1,478,557
2	Paul Azinger	1,458,456
3	Greg Norman	1,359,653
4	Jim Gallagher Jr	1,078,870
5	David Frost	1,030,717
6	Payne Stewart	982,875
7	Lee Janzen	932,335
8	Tom Kite	887,811
9	Fulton Allem	851,345
10	Fred Couples	796,579
11	Jeff Maggert	793,023
12	Davis Love III	777,059
13	Larry Mize	724,660
14	Scott Simpson	707,166
15	John Huston	681,441
16	Rocco Mediate	680,623
17	Steve Elkington	675,383
18	Corey Pavin	675,087
19	Vijay Singh	657,831
20	David Edwards	653,086
21	Mark Calcavecchia	630,366
22	Phil Mickelson	628,735
23	Bernhard Langer	626,938
24	Gil Morgan	610,312
25	Chip Beck	603,376
26	Jay Haas	601,603
27	Jim McGovern	587,495
28	Rick Fehr	556,322
29	Craig Stadler	553,623
30	Billy Mayfair	513,072
31	Nolan Henke	502,375
32	Bob Estes	447,187
33	Tom Lehman	422,761
34	Howard Twitty	416,833
35	Grant Waite	411,405
36	Dan Forsman	410,150
37	Scott Hoch	403,742
38	Joey Sindelar	391,649
39	Fuzzy Zoeller	378,175
40	Billy Andrade	365,759
41	Mark McCumber	363,269
42	Mark Wiebe	360,213
43	Mark O'Meara	349,516
44	Keith Clearwater	348,763
45	John Cook	342,321
46	Tom Watson	342,023
47	Donnie Hammond	340,432
48	Brett Ogle	337,374
49	Mike Standly	323,886
50	Craig Parry	323,068
51	Ben Crenshaw	318,605
52	Dudley Hart	316,750
53	Loren Roberts	316,506
54	Bob Lohr	314,982
55	Brad Faxon	312,023
56	Fred Funk	309,435
57	Bill Glasson	299,799
58	D A Weibring	299,293
59	Russ Cochran	293,868
60	Greg Kraft	290,581
61	Blaine McCallister	290,434
62	Andrew Magee	269,986
63	Curtis Strange	262,697
64	Steve Pate	254,841
65	Hale Irwin	252,686
66	Mark Brooks	249,696
67	Dave Rummells	247,963
68	Lanny Wadkins	244,544
69	John Inman	242,140
70	Robert Gamez	236,458
71	Jay Delsing	233,484
72	Greg Twiggs	231,823
73	Michael Allen	231,072
74	Brad Bryant	230,139
75	Ken Green	229,750
76	John Daly	225,591
77	Peter Jacobsen	222,291
78	John Adams	221,753
79	Mike Springer	214,729
80	Richard Zokol	214,419
81	Bruce Fleisher	214,279
82	Dick Mast	210,125
83	Phil Blackmar	207,310
84	Duffy Waldorf	202,638
85	Brian Claar	202,624
86	Jay Don Blake	202,482
87	Tom Sieckmann	201,429
88	Kenny Perry	196,863
89	Mike Hulbert	193,833
90	Kirk Triplett	189,418
91	Nick Faldo	188,886
92	Steve Lowery	188,287
93	Jeff Sluman	187,841
94	Brian Kamm	183,185
95	Wayne Levi	179,521
96	Dave Barr	179,264
97	Billy Ray Brown	173,662
98	Dillard Pruitt	168,053
99	Ed Dougherty	167,651
100	Ted Schulz	164,260

1993 LPGA Tour Review

It is true... everything comes to she who waits

It was easy to lose count of the number of times last year that Betsy King went into the final round of an LPGA Tour event either leading, or sharing the lead, only to be overtaken on the last day. It happened in the first Major of the year, the Nabisco Dinah Shore at Mission Hills in California and it happened in the fourth and final Major of the year, the du Maurier Classic in Canada. A Swedish player did it to her, an English player, a Japanese player – even some of her close friends left her high and dry, but finally, at the last hole of the last event of the season it all came right. Betsy King holed a 20 foot birdie putt for a round of 67 to win the Toray Japan Queens Cup, her first LPGA title of 1993. Not only must she have felt mightily relieved but with her win (worth $97,500) she overtook Patty Sheehan to finish the year as Leading Moneywinner with $595,992 and surged past Brandie Burton to claim the Rolex LPGA Player of the Year Award. Talk about leaving it late!

A great year for King (in the end) but perhaps an even more momentous or more historic one for Sheehan and, in terms of future significance, a more telling one for Burton. 1993 was also a remarkable year for the Swedish, English and Japanese players on the LPGA Tour.

History was made at Moon Valley in Phoenix. It was there in the third week of March that Patty Sheehan won the Standard Register Ping tournament by five shots. As this was the 30th LPGA victory of her career it gave Sheehan entry into the LPGA's Hall of Fame, an honour previously achieved by only 12 players. Winning the Money List would have been a 'considerable bonus' but that came anyway when she won the 1993 Mazda

(Right) England's Trish Johnson won successive LPGA tournaments in April. (Above inset) Brandie Burton claimed her first Major last year and Betsy King (opposite) became the season's Leading Moneywinner with a last gasp effort in Japan

LPGA Championship – her fifth Major (if one includes her 1992 British Open victory) – at Bethesda in June.

Twenty-one year old Brandie Burton also won one of the LPGA Majors in 1993 – the first of several in the unanimous opinion of those who have followed her short but brilliant career. Burton won the du Maurier Classic at the London Hunt Club in Ontario after a play-off with King, and just like King's end-of-season victory, it was secured with a 20 foot birdie putt. She also won the Jamie Farr Toledo Classic and Safeco tournaments (becoming the only Tour player to achieve three wins) and gained 16 top 10 finishes in the 26 events she entered to take third place on the Money List. Gracious in defeat at the du Maurier, King said of her young rival: 'She is probably going to win more tournaments than anyone in the next ten years'.

Dottie Mochrie may have something to say about King's assessment. She was the player who dominated the LPGA Tour in 1992 but until an October win in the World Championship of Women's Golf, 1993 had been a frustrating year. She won lots of money

(Above) Patty Sheehan wins the Mazda LPGA Championship. (Right) Dottie Mochrie had to wait until October for her first victory in 1993

and regularly finished high on the final leaderboard but Mochrie has a 'second place is no place' type mentality. Losing a five hole play-off to the English rookie Helen Dobson in the State Farm Rail Classic in September must have rankled immensely and probably fired her up for that overdue success in Florida.

Of a different temperament altogether are Meg Mallon, Tammie Green and the forever smiling and rapidly improving Japanese player, Hiromi Kobayashi, all of whom joined Sheehan as two-time winners. Talking of smiling faces, the great Nancy Lopez eagled the last hole of the Youngstown-Warren LPGA

Lauri Merten tamed Crooked Stick and overtook Helen Alfredsson to win the US Women's Open

Classic to force a play-off with Deb Richard, then promptly birdied the first sudden death hole to record her 47th career victory.

Laura Davies has become a Nancy Lopez-like figure of European golf and her victory in the McDonald's Championship in May put the seal on an incredible Spring for European golfers in America. Just as Bernhard Langer won the Masters at Augusta, the men's first Major championship of 1993, so Sweden's Helen Alfredsson won the Nabisco Dinah Shore at Mission Hills in March. It was Alfredsson's first American victory in only her second season on Tour; in 1992 she was the LPGA's Rookie of the Year. (Her successor in 1993, incidentally, was the English player, Suzanne Strudwick).

Within seven days of Alfredsson's triumph, Britain's Trish Johnson won the next event in Las Vegas (her first LPGA title) and followed that with a victory in the Atlanta Championship. Johnson was the only player in 1993 to win successive tournaments. Then, just when it was beginning to look as if the overseas tide had been turned back, Alfredsson came within the proverbial whisker of winning the US Women's Open Championship at Crooked Stick.

The emotional Swede led by two shots after three rounds but was finally caught on the back nine by Lauri Merten, who chipped-in from 25 yards for a birdie at the 70th hole and went on to become a surprise – though hugely popular – winner of the most important championship in women's golf.

Merten had hinted that she was in good form a month earlier, when closing rounds of 66-67 lifted her into second place behind Sheehan in the LPGA Championship, but the US Open was her first win in almost nine years. King, therefore, wasn't the only player to prove in 1993 that 'everything comes to she who waits'.

THE 1993 LPGA MAJORS

25 - 28 March

Nabisco Dinah Shore

MISSIONS HILLS, RANCHO MIRAGE, CALIFORNIA

H Alfredsson	69	71	72	72	284	$105000
A Benz	72	73	71	70	286	49901
T Barrett	70	73	72	71	286	49901
B King	71	74	67	74	286	49901
H Stacy	72	74	71	70	287	25126
M Berteotti	68	74	73	72	287	25126
D Coe-Jones	72	68	72	75	287	25126
N Lopez	68	78	72	70	288	15762
B Burton	73	73	68	74	288	15762
T Johnson	74	68	72	74	288	15762
J Crafter	71	72	70	75	288	15762

Helen Alfredsson wins her first major championship at Mission Hills

10 - 13 June

Mazda LPGA Championship

BETHESDA, MARYLAND

P Sheehan	68	68	70	69	275	$150000
L Merten	73	70	66	67	276	93093
B Bunkowsky	68	70	69	70	277	67933
B King	72	66	72	69	279	40130
M McGann	73	68	68	70	279	40130
T Green	71	69	69	70	279	40130
P Rizzo	72	69	67	71	279	40130
N Scranton	74	68	72	66	280	23651
T Johnson	68	73	69	70	280	23651
C Johnson	68	68	70	74	280	23651

22 - 25 July

48th US Women's Open

CROOKED STICK, CARMEL, INDIANA

L Merten	71	71	70	68	280	$144000
D Andrews	71	70	69	71	281	62431
H Alfredsson	68	70	69	74	281	62431
P Bradley	72	70	68	73	283	29249
H Kobayashi	71	67	71	74	283	29249
P Sheehan	73	71	69	71	284	22379
B King	74	70	72	69	285	17525
M McGann	70	66	78	71	285	17525
N Lopez	70	71	70	74	285	17525
A Okamoto	68	72	71	74	285	17525
L Davies	73	71	69	73	286	13993
J Carner	71	69	73	73	286	13993

26 - 29 August

Du Maurier Ltd Classic

LONDON HUNT, ONTARIO, CANADA

B Burton	71	70	66	70	277	$120000
B King	65	70	71	71	277	74,474
(Burton won sudden-death play-off)						
D Coe-Jones	64	74	72	68	278	54346
D Mochrie	68	69	71	71	279	42269
K Monaghan	72	71	71	66	280	31198
V Fergon	67	73	68	72	280	31198
D Lofland-Dormann	68	68	73	72	281	23751
H Alfredsson	70	70	72	70	282	19926
K Guadagnino	69	69	70	74	282	19926
D Ammaccapane	72	72	73	66	283	14894
S Steinhauer	73	69	71	70	283	14894
J Dickinson	70	71	71	71	283	14894

THE 1993 LPGA TOUR

TOURNAMENT · WINNERS

HealthSouth Palm Beach Classic	Tammie Green
Itoki Hawaiian Ladies Open	Lisa Walters
Ping/Welch's Championship	Meg Mallon
Standard Register Ping	Patty Sheehan
Nabisco Dinah Shore	Helen Alfredsson
Las Vegas International	Trish Johnson
Atlanta Women's Championship	Trish Johnson
Sprint Classic	Kristi Albers
Sara Lee Classic	Meg Mallon
McDonald's Championship	Laura Davies
Lady Keystone Open	Val Skinner
LPGA Corning Classic	Kelly Robbins
JCPenney/LPGA Skins Game	Betsy King
Oldsmobile Classic	Jane Geddes
Mazda LPGA Championship	Patty Sheehan
Rochester International	Tammie Green
ShopRite Classic	Shelley Hamlin
Jamie Farr Toledo Classic	Brandie Burton
Youngstown-Warren Classic	Nancy Lopez
JAL Big Apple Classic	Hiromi Kobayashi
US Women's Open	Lauri Merten
Ping/Welch's Classic	Missie Berteotti
McCall's LPGA Classic at Stratton Mountain	Dana Lofland-Dormann
Sun-Times Challenge	Cindy Schreyer
Minnesota Classic	Hiromi Kobayashi
du Maurier Ltd Classic	Brandie Burton
State Farm Rail Charity Classic	Helen Dobson
Ping-Cellular One Championship	Donna Andrews
Safeco Classic	Brandie Burton
Kyocera Inamori Classic	Kris Monaghan
World Championship of Women's Golf	Dottie Mochrie
Nichirei International	US LPGA bt Japan LPGA 23-9
Toray Japan Queens Cup	Betsy King

LEADING · MONEY · WINNERS

1	Betsy King	$595,992
2	Patty Sheehan	540,547
3	Brandie Burton	517,741
4	Dottie Mochrie	429,118
5	Helen Alfredsson	402,685
6	Lauri Merten	394,744
7	Tammie Green	356,579
8	Hiromi Kobayashi	347,060
9	Donna Andrews	334,285
10	Trish Johnson	331,745
11	Rosie Jones	320,964
12	Michelle McGann	315,921
13	Sherri Steinhauer	311,967
14	Nancy Lopez	304,480
15	Meg Mallon	276,294
16	Dawn Coe-Jones	271,978
17	Kristi Albers	263,483
18	Jane Geddes	263,149
19	Tina Barrett	261,249
20	Laura Davies	240,643
21	D. Lofland-Dormann	234,415
22	Deb Richard	223,282
23	Kris Monaghan	208,987
24	Kelly Robbins	200,744
25	Kris Tschetter	196,913
26	Hollis Stacy	191,257
27	Pat Bradley	188,135
28	D Ammaccapane	187,862
29	Jane Crafter	187,190
30	Judy Dickinson	186,317
31	Missie Berteotti	184,553
32	Missie McGeorge	180,311
33	Elaine Crosby	177,726
34	Cindy Rarick	174,407
35	Amy Benz	166,968
36	Jan Stephenson	161,123
37	Lisa Walters	149,260
38	Dale Eggeling	145,789
39	Barb Bunkowsky	142,907
40	Beth Daniel	140,001
41	JoAnne Carner	134,956
42	Nancy Scranton	129,766
43	Val Skinner	129,665
44	Shelley Hamlin	129,447
45	Gail Graham	126,048
46	Mary Zimmerman	118,626
47	Juli Inkster	116,583
48	Alice Ritzman	113,992
49	Patti Rizzo	111,371
50	Chris Johnson	111,027

AUSTRALASIA

1993 Australasian Tour Review

From Allenby to Diaz: the year Down Under began with an 'A' and ended with a 'z'

Nineteen ninety three was an incredible year for Australian golf. It was a memorable one in many respects but if we learned anything it was that we should throw away those crystal balls and accept that golf is the most unpredictable of games. Mind you, we were given misleading signals at the very beginning.

Four days of golf tricked us into believing that 1993 was going to pick up where 1992 left off. For the first time in several years the Australasian Tour didn't commence its schedule in January on the Gold Coast of Queensland, instead it made an early return to Royal Melbourne for the Tournament Players Championship. The great course had staged the Johnnie Walker Classic in the previous December and when Robert Allenby repeated his victory in that event, it seemed certain that the 21 year-old rising star would go on to dominate the domestic scene and retain his Leading Moneywinners title.

Allenby even produced a near carbon copy winning score, as in the December event he produced rounds of 66-68-69-72 for a total of 275, and in the TPC he scored 71-66-69-68 for an aggregate of 274.

The other presumption concerning

(Pages 156-157) Royal Pines, Queensland; (right) Peter Senior, Robert Allenby and Greg Norman at the Heineken Classic in Perth

Australian golf was that during his sporadic returns home, Greg Norman would feature prominently in the events he entered but on the international scene would again be found wanting in the Majors. How wrong could we be?

Allenby had a reasonable season in 1993 but after his success in Melbourne the anticipated haul of victories failed to materialise and by the end of the year he had relinquished his Order of Merit crown. The adventures of Greg Norman in the 1993 Majors could probably fill a book on their own but his performances Down Under were largely forgettable. The reality was that both Allenby, and Norman when in Australia, were eclipsed by a combination of Peter Senior, broom-handled putters and visiting Americans.

Bradley Hughes, winner of the 1993 Australian Masters at Huntingdale

The second event of 1993 was the Heineken Classic at the Vines Resort near Perth. Huge crowds turned up to watch Norman playing with Allenby in the first round and the same went away having seen the third member of their group – one Peter Senior – steel their thunder with a marvellous round of 65. Senior also 'stole' the tournament, although that word is hardly appropriate given that he led from start to finish and gave a superb exhibition of golf.

Peter Fowler won the Australian circuit's next event, the New Zealand Open by two strokes at windy Paraparaumu, and then it was 'Gold Jacket time' with the Australian Masters at Huntingdale. Given his outstanding record in the event, the failure of six-time champion Greg Norman to make an impression was surprising, but what happened to Peter Senior at Huntingdale almost defies belief. In the first round he scored a 68, including a hole-in-one, for which his reward was $100,000; on Day Two he ballooned to an awful 78 but then followed it with another of those spectacular 65s, the highlight of his round being an amazing seven successive birdies. It gave him a three stroke lead going into the final day and when Senior reached the 18th green on Sunday he faced two putts for a one shot victory and his second Masters title in three years. Somehow – and he claimed he was upset by flashing cameras – he contrived to three putt; a play-off against Bradley Hughes was the result, and the result of that was a defeat for Senior. It was Hughes' first big win in Australia and a week's golf that Peter Senior will never forget. The final extraordinary fact about the 1993 Masters was that the first three finishers in the tournament, Hughes, Senior and Terry Price all putted with the controversial broom-handled putter. And yes, there were more than a few mutterings from more than a few quarters.

Before the Australasian Tour completed the first half of its 1993 schedule (traditionally there is a lengthy break between March and October) the New Zealand golfer Michael Campbell provided another big story.

In the Canon Challenge event at Castle Hill, Robert Allenby stormed to an opening 63 but was first overtaken and then, like the rest of the cast in Sydney, comprehensively beaten by the young Maori golfer who surged through the field with middle rounds of 65-65 before cruising to a comfortable victory on the final day. It was not the strongest line-up of the year but no lesser a judge than Ray Floyd has described the 1992 Australian Amateur champion as the best young player he has ever seen and the Canon Challenge was only the fifth professional event of Campbell's career.

The Americans who won Down Under in 1993: (left) Brad Faxon and (opposite) Curtis Strange

Tournaments in Singapore and Malaysia were staged on either side of the mid season interval, with wins being achieved by Paul Moloney in the former and Anthony Painter in the latter, and in the first week of November Wayne Smith claimed the Eagle Blue Open title at Royal Adelaide. Smith won a three way play-off at the third extra hole in an event reduced to three rounds after the first day was abandoned due to freak winds. (Not so much a case of crystal balls as oscillating balls.)

Next came the Australian PGA Championship at Concord and a spectacular triumph for The Shark. No, not he of the Great White variety but the one that people started to call the Tall, Dark, Hyphenated Shark after his victory in the 1991 British Open at Royal Birkdale – and whose form since has been extremely patchy. Ian Baker-Finch started the final round of the 'PGA nine behind third round leader Peter Fowler but played the first nine holes in 29 strokes – just as he had done at Royal Birkdale.

He finished with a 64 which eventually tied him with Fowler and New Zealand's Grant Waite. The elegant Baker-Finch completed his remarkable comeback by winning the championship with a birdie at the second extra hole.

After such a performance, the popular Baker-Finch was one of the favourites to win the Heineken Australian Open at Metropolitan in late November. The event is reviewed ahead, suffice to say here that neither of the 'Aussie Sharks' was at his best: Baker-Finch, opened with a promising 67, but then returned to being 'patchy', scoring a 78 in the second round, while Greg Norman failed to break 70 in each of the four rounds.

Metropolitan saw the first part of the great American double act. Brad Faxon's win in Melbourne was immediately followed by Curtis Strange's victory in the inaugural Greg Norman Holden Classic at The Lakes. 'A great friend of mine came out of a slump today', Norman said after Strange had gained his first tournament success since the 1989 US Open. He did it in some style too, producing rounds of 68-67-69-70 in wet and windy conditions, over one of the toughest courses in Australia. Strange's 274 total was six better than Steve Elkington managed in the 1992 Heineken Australian Open, also played at The Lakes.

It seemed likely that a third successive

American victory would occur in the Tour's penultimate event, the Air New Zealand/Shell Open. Brad Faxon was the major attraction at The Grange in Auckland, and following a first round 65 looked set to complete a famous Australia – New Zealand double. On Sunday afternoon Faxon was still in with a good chance of winning before Terry Price scraped home by a single shot. Faxon shared second place with Wayne Riley and the fast-finishing Michael Campbell.

There was still one tournament to go, and time for a final surprise before Christmas. Coolum on the Sunshine Coast was the place to be and, although Peter Senior had already been assured of capturing the Order of Merit title, the likes of Robert Allenby, Ian Baker-

Ian Baker-Finch scored a brilliant 64 in his final round to win the Australian PGA Championship

Finch, Rodger Davis and Craig Parry were determined to prevent him from finishing on a winning note. For three days, however, Peter Senior looked as if he was heading for precisely that until the hitherto unheard-of David Diaz snatched the title with a 67 on the final day. Senior, who was supposed to shoot the 67, scored a 76, but then it was that kind of year. Any predictions for 1994?

HEINEKEN AUSTRALIAN OPEN

ROLL · OF · HONOUR

Year	Winner
1904	Michael Scott (Am)
1905	Dan Soutar
1906	Carnegie Clark
1907	Michael Scott (Am)
1908	Clyde Pearce (Am)
1909	Claude Felstead (Am)
1910	Carnegie Clark
1911	Carnegie Clark
1912	Ivo Whitton (Am)
1913	Ivo Whitton (Am)
1914-19	no championship
1920	Joe Kirkwood
1921	Arthur Le Fevre
1922	Charles Campbell
1923	Tom Howard
1924	Alex Russell (Am)
1925	Fred Popplewell
1926	Ivo Whitton (Am)
1927	Rufus Stewart
1928	Fred Popplewell
1929	Ivo Whitton (Am)
1930	Francis Eyre
1931	Ivo Whitton (Am)
1932	Mick Ryan (Am)
1933	Lou Kelly
1934	Bill Bolger
1935	F W McMahon
1936	Gene Sarazen
1937	George Naismith
1938	Jim Ferrier (Am)
1939	Jim Ferrier (Am)
1940-45	no championship
1946	Ossie Pickworth
1947	Ossie Pickworth
1948	Ossie Pickworth
1949	Eric Cremin
1950	Norman von Nida
1951	Peter Thomson
1952	Norman von Nida
1953	Norman von Nida
1954	Ossie Pickworth
1955	Bobby Locke
1956	Bruce Crampton
1957	Frank Phillips
1958	Gary Player
1959	Kel Nagle
1960	Bruce Devlin (Am)
1961	Frank Phillips
1962	Gary Player
1963	Gary Player
1964	Jack Nicklaus
1965	Gary Player
1966	Arnold Palmer
1967	Peter Thomson
1968	Jack Nicklaus
1969	Gary Player
1970	Gary Player
1971	Jack Nicklaus
1972	Peter Thomson
1973	J C Snead
1974	Gary Player
1975	Jack Nicklaus
1976	Jack Nicklaus
1977	David Graham
1978	Jack Nicklaus
1979	Jack Newton
1980	Greg Norman
1981	Bill Rogers
1982	Bob Shearer
1983	Peter Fowler
1984	Tom Watson
1985	Greg Norman
1986	Rodger Davis
1987	Greg Norman
1988	Mark Calcavecchia
1989	Peter Senior
1990	John Morse
1991	Wayne Riley
1992	Steve Elkington
1993	Brad Faxon

1993 Heineken Australian Open

Metropolitan GC, Melbourne, November 25 - 28

Australia has always been a generous nation. Year after year it stages a splendid national golf championship on a splendid natural golf course; the sun shines all week long, large crowds appear and an American walks off with the trophy. Well, maybe not every year.

Americans have been winning Australia's Open Championship since the 1930s and the days of Gene Sarazen. The same Gene Sarazen, that is, who at a sprightly 91 years of age told Greg Norman at last year's British Open that his victory was the greatest championship performance he had ever seen. As Gene Sarazen won his one and only Australian title at Melbourne's Metropolitan Golf Club in 1936, it would have made a nice story if Greg Norman could have rounded off his extraordinary year with a win over the same course in the 1993 Heineken Australian Open.

Greg had played in the two most recent Opens at Metropolitan: in 1979 he came second to Jack Newton (after missing a putt to win at the final hole), and in 1986 when, as with last year, he was the reigning British Open champion, he tied for seventh.

Greg Norman, of course, didn't win his fourth Australian championship in 1993, the American Brad Faxon did (or Bradford John Faxon Jnr, to be precise). Faxon beat the cream of Australian golf – not to mention his fellow overseas challengers, such as Ray Floyd, Curtis Strange and Sandy Lyle – because he played brilliantly in his first and third rounds and because when things didn't go his way in the second and final rounds he remained patient and kept his nerve. The fact that for four days he putted like Bob Charles didn't do him any harm either.

Faxon got off to a terrific start on Thursday. Recent changes to the course had given Metropolitan a reputation as one of the more difficult of Melbourne's many great sandbelt courses. The fairways are not as generous as they are at a few of the neighbouring layouts but the putting surfaces are invariably just as quick and certainly equally lethal. Venturing too far off the fairways is not to be recommended either at

The 18th green at Metropolitan

Metropolitan for the rough can be penal and the woodland is as dense as it is attractive. Faxon rarely missed the centre of the fairway on the opening day but it was his skill on those 'lethal' greens that mostly enabled him to equal Greg Norman's 10 year-old course record.

This hugely impressive score of 65 gave Faxon a two stroke lead over Ian Baker-Finch, Peter Senior and New Zealand's Grant Waite. It also brought the American a nine stroke advantage over his first round playing partner, Greg Norman. To be fair at once to The Shark, for two days or more Norman had been suffering from severe stomach cramps. The pain was apparently later relieved by taking 'a secret potion sent to him by a lady in Darwin'. Whatever were its ingredients, it helped Norman to survive the halfway cut and complete the tournament but he was never a serious contender. As for the defending champion Steve Elkington, the 'All-American Aussie', as the Texas resident but New South Wales born player was christened after his triumph at The Lakes in 1992, couldn't discover his best form either. He scored a fine

Neither Ray Floyd (above) nor defending champion Steve Elkington (right) was able to mount a serious challenge

Brad Faxon wins at Metropolitan. "I'm thrilled to death", the American said after claiming a two stroke victory (full result on page 167)

68 in the final round but by then it was much too late.

On a wild and windy second day Faxon dropped three shots at the last two holes and lost his lead to the little-known David Iwasaka-Smith. He bounced back immediately in the third round, however, with birdies at the 1st, 3rd and 4th holes en route to an excellent 66. It was a score that nobody could better on Saturday and with a three round total of 205 (11 under par) Faxon once again held a two stroke advantage, this time over Wayne Grady, Jeff Woodland and the local favourite, Melbourne's Robert Allenby.

With rounds of 70-69-68 Allenby had been steadily climbing towards the top of the leaderboard. After a barren spell he was clearly playing well again and impartial observers rated him as the most likely Australian player to challenge Faxon in Sunday's final round. Wayne Grady, Rodger Davis and Peter Senior, respectively two, three and four shots behind the American were the other major 'home hopes' that people mentioned.

It proved to be an exciting final day. Faxon started strongly with a birdie at the 4th and an eagle at the 6th but he was soon being chased by a posse of Australians. Surprisingly, Allenby wasn't one of them, and perhaps more surprisingly, it was the unsung Queenslander Jeff Woodland together with Michael Clayton, a one-time junior golfer at Metropolitan, who led the pursuit. Playing well ahead of Faxon, Clayton (6 shots behind overnight) scored two eagles on the front nine and set a good target for the others when he birdied the 14th, 17th and 18th holes in a round of 66. Woodland drew level with Faxon at the 12th and as they played the 17th they were still level, one ahead of Clayton.

Enter now the 'Bob Charles of American golf'. Faxon rolled in a 35 foot putt for a birdie at the penultimate hole as Woodland three-putted from just off the green. This was the decisive moment; both players parred the final hole, Faxon thus achieving his victory by two strokes. Woodland tied Clayton for second place and Senior and Grady finished a further shot back in joint fourth position.

Another American champion for Metropolitan – another fine championship for Australia. Roll on Royal Sydney.

THE 1993 AUSTRALASIAN TOUR

January 21st - 24th

TOURNAMENT PLAYERS CHAMPIONSHIP

ROYAL MELBOURNE

R Allenby	71	66	69	68	274	Aus$54,000
W Grady	70	72	65	67	274	32,400
(Allenby won play-off at first extra hole)						
R Mackay	72	68	68	69	277	20,700
P O'Malley	73	71	69	66	279	14,940
P Senior	75	66	69	70	280	12,480
P Teravainen	71	68	70	72	281	11,460
M Campbell	69	71	74	69	283	8,595
W Riley	74	71	68	70	283	8,595
S Appleby	69	70	72	72	283	8,595
P McWhinney	70	70	70	73	283	8,595
I Baker-Finch	71	68	72	74	285	5,480
O Moore	70	70	73	72	285	5,480
S Rintoul	70	71	74	70	285	5,480

January 28th - 31st

HEINEKEN CLASSIC

THE VINES, PERTH

P Senior	65	71	67	72	275	Aus$54,000
M Campbell	70	69	72	67	278	32,400
R Allenby	67	70	71	71	279	20,400
L Wastle	73	70	69	68	280	12,400
S Appleby	71	68	72	69	280	12,400
P O'Malley	68	70	68	74	280	12,400
G Joyner	70	68	71	72	281	9,900
T Price	72	69	75	66	282	8,800
L Stephen	68	68	75	71	282	8,800
G Norman	72	70	73	69	284	7,350
W Grady	75	70	66	73	284	7,350
J Freeman	69	72	69	74	284	7,350
L Brown	73	69	76	67	285	5,700
J Kay	70	71	72	72	285	5,700
M Clayton	68	72	69	76	285	5,700

February 18th - 21st

AUSTRALIAN MASTERS

HUNTINGDALE

B Hughes	70	72	73	66	281	Aus$130,572
P Senior	68	78	65	70	281	73,990
(Hughes won play-off at first extra hole)						
T Price	68	74	72	70	284	48,964
C Parry	67	79	69	70	285	34,819
M Allen	69	76	71	70	286	29,016
G Norman	71	74	70	72	287	26,114
N Price	73	70	78	67	288	22,124
R Davis	77	70	71	70	288	22,124
S Leaney	69	77	71	72	289	19,585
W Grady	71	74	76	69	290	14,798
B Jones	74	74	73	69	290	14,798
A Gilligan	72	76	72	70	290	14,798
I Baker-Finch	73	74	72	71	290	14,798
R Allenby	73	74	71	72	290	14,798

Peter Senior, winner in 1993 of the Heineken Classic and the Order of Merit

November 18th - 21st

FORD AUSTRALIAN PGA CHAMPIONSHIP

CONCORD, SYDNEY

I Baker-Finch	69	69	73	64	275	Aus$63,000
P Fowler	71	64	67	73	275	29,662
G Waite	66	69	73	67	275	29,662
(Baker-Finch won play-off at second extra hole)						
J Payne	71	67	73	66	277	15,400
J Morse	68	67	70	72	277	15,400
W Riley	71	68	71	68	278	12,600
B Hughes	75	68	68	68	279	10,266
C Parry	68	72	70	69	279	10,266
R Whitlock	70	68	69	72	279	10,266
L Wastle	73	68	72	67	280	6,361
W Smith	71	71	71	67	280	6,361
M Harwood	74	66	72	68	280	6,361
J Woodland	66	72	73	69	280	6,361
J Clifford	68	71	71	70	280	6,361
B Ogle	65	69	71	75	280	6,361

November 25th - 28th

HEINEKEN AUSTRALIAN OPEN

METROPOLITAN, MELBOURNE

B Faxon	65	74	66	70	275	Aus$153,000
J Woodland	71	68	68	70	277	73,037
M Clayton	69	71	71	66	277	73,037
P Senior	67	73	69	69	278	37,400
W Grady	68	69	70	71	278	37,400
G Waite	67	73	68	72	280	30,600
R Davis	70	70	69	73	282	27,200
W Smith	70	72	70	72	284	24,650
Z Zorkic	72	75	70	68	285	19,040
L Stephen	69	73	71	72	285	19,040
C Strange	69	74	72	70	285	19,040
R Allenby	70	69	68	78	285	19,040
M Harwood	77	69	71	68	285	19,040
C Gray	71	71	70	74	286	11,850
S Elkington	72	74	72	68	286	11,850
P Devenport	70	75	66	75	286	11,850
M Ferguson	69	74	68	75	286	11,850
R Floyd	71	73	71	71	286	11,850
B Ogle	71	70	73	72	286	11,850

TOURNAMENT · WINNERS

Tournament Players Championship	Robert Allenby
Heineken Classic	Peter Senior
AMP New Zealand Open	Peter Fowler
Microsoft Australian Masters	Bradley Hughes
Canon Challenge	Michael Campbell
Epson Singapore Open	Paul Moloney
Meru Valley Perak Masters	Anthony Painter
Victorian Open	Lucas Parsons
Eagle Blue Open	Wayne Smith
Australian PGA Championship	Ian Baker-Finch
Heineken Australian Open	Brad Faxon
Greg Norman Holden Classic	Curtis Strange
Air New Zealand/Shell Open	Terry Price
Coolum Classic	David Diaz

1993 ORDER OF MERIT: TOP 25

1	Peter Senior	Aus $243,504
2	Bradley Hughes	190,147
3	Robert Allenby	171,083
4	Paul Moloney	134,694
5	Mike Clayton	131,034
6	Terry Price	120,148
7	Michael Campbell	117,168
8	John Wade	116,501
9	Wayne Grady	93,812
10	Peter Fowler	93,416
11	Jeff Woodland	92,227
12	Ian Baker-Finch	92,047
13	Wayne Smith	89,308
14	Richard Green	86,213
15	Peter O'Malley	59,663
16	Mike Harwood	59,613
17	Wayne Riley	56,337
18	Craig Parry	52,098
19	Paul Devenport	50,242
20	Zoran Zorkic	49,148
21	Jeff Wagner	48,911
22	Lucas Parsons	48,349
23	John Morse	47,551
24	Anthony Gilligan	47,075
25	John Clifford	45,508

JAPAN

ional Tour
Taiheiyo

1993 Japanese Tour Review

For once it wasn't so much the things he did achieve but more the things he did not. That's what everyone was talking about. We are reviewing golf in Japan which means we are discussing the life and times of 'Jumbo' Masashi Ozaki.

For some time now, 'Jumbo' has been to Japanese golf what Arnold Palmer was to American golf in the 1960s and Seve Ballesteros to European golf in the 1980s. In 20 seasons he has won more than 80 tournaments and has led the Japanese Order of Merit seven times. Right up until the beginning of December last year it was assumed that he would increase that number to eight – he didn't. That was one of his 'failures'. The second was the uncharacteristic habit he developed of throwing away clear winning opportunities. It happened on several occasions in 1993 and had the same occurred as frequently to any other player one might have heard – and heaven forbid it should ever be uttered in 'Jumbo's' presence – the word 'choke'. It was Hajime Meshiai who captured the Japanese Order of Merit (or Leading Moneywinner title) at the end of 1993, after a marvellous year-long battle with Ozaki for the number one position.

Meshiai started the season well with two early victories. 'Jumbo' responded by finishing joint runner-up to Peter Senior in the Chunichi Crowns and winning the Fuji Sankei Classic and the Japan PGA Championship in successive weeks. During a fairly quiet summer Meshiai regained the initiative but with most of the major events taking place towards the end of the season, starting with 'Jumbo's' defence of the Japan Open in early October, the great man seemed perfectly placed to overhaul his less-gifted countryman. It was now, however, that the uncharacteristic and ultimately fatal flaw crept into 'Jumbo's' game.

After three rounds of the Japan Open Championship, 'Jumbo' led the field by two

The price of fame! 'Jumbo' Ozaki has become a golfing icon in Japan

(Far left) Hajime Meshiai proved to be a thorn in the side of 'Jumbo' Ozaki throughout 1993. (Left) Greg Norman wins the Taiheiyo Masters

shots. He had scored 69-72-69 but on the final day struggled to a 76, allowing Seiki Okuda to win the most important title of his career. 'Jumbo' immediately won his next event, the Asahi Beer Digest but in the two following tournaments he posted final rounds of 75 and 76, the latter allowing Meshiai to once again take the lead in the Order of Merit.

November in Japan traditionally brings the 'invasion' of the bounty hunters from Europe, America and elsewhere. It is the season of the International Tour, a lucrative trio of events comprising the Taiheiyo Masters, Dunlop Phoenix and Casio World Open tournaments.

Top overseas players regularly win these events, and 1993 was no exception. Greg Norman eagled the 72nd hole at the Taiheiyo Masters to snatch a dramatic victory; Ernie Els played 'the best golf of my life' to win the Dunlop Phoenix by four shots and Tom Lehman got the better of Phil Mickelson over the closing holes in the Casio World Open at Ibusuki. So where was the mighty 'Jumbo'? He was there, all right. He led going into the final round of the Taiheiyo Masters but finished 3rd; he was a stroke behind Ernie Els after three rounds of the Dunlop Phoenix but tied with four others for second place and though never in a winning position in the Casio event, a poor finish cost him a significant number of Yen and, more importantly, the chance of catching Meshiai at the top of the Money List.

'Jumbo' gave himself one final opportunity to put matters right when he entered the Japan Series at Yomiuri, Tokyo (his Tour's equivalent of the Tour Championship in America or Volvo Masters in Europe). Everything went right for three rounds and he looked to be cruising to a famous victory – a victory that would provide the perfect answer to his critics – when suddenly the wheels fell off. After scores of 68-66-68 he slipped to a 72; not only did this enable old adversary Tommy Nakajima to collect his second tournament win of the year but it also allowed Meshiai, who finished strongly with a 67, to finally secure the Order of Merit crown.

Norman's late collapse in San Francisco; 'Monty's' last gasp victory at Valderrama to deny Faldo and now 'Jumbo's' slip-up in Tokyo. Thus were the mighty felled in 1993.

JAPAN'S 1993 INTERNATIONAL TOUR

11 - 14 November

SUMITOMO VISA TAIHEIYO MASTERS

GOTEMBA

G Norman	70	67	67	68	272	Y27,000,000
Y Mizumaki	67	68	68	70	273	15,000,000
D Frost	68	71	70	65	274	7,800,000
B Lane	68	70	68	68	274	7,800,000
M Ozaki	66	69	67	72	274	7,800,000
T Nakajima	70	68	69	69	276	5,400,000
I Aoki	71	70	66	71	278	4,350,000
I Baker-Finch	71	66	70	71	278	4,350,000
J Sluman	71	69	66	72	278	4,350,000
C Parry	71	70	70	68	279	3,450,000
B Franklin	70	70	71	69	280	3,000,000
T Hamilton	70	70	72	69	281	2,640,000
H Hamano	74	69	66	72	281	2,640,000
I Shirahama	72	72	70	68	282	1,800,700
B Watts	72	70	72	68	282	1,800,700
S Higashi	72	69	73	68	282	1,800,700
H Miyase	74	69	70	69	282	1,800,700
T-C Chen	68	70	74	70	282	1,800,700
K Suzuki	72	69	71	70	282	1,800,700
K Hasegama	72	68	71	71	282	1,800,700
K Takahashi	72	68	70	72	282	1,800,700

18 - 21 November

DUNLOP PHOENIX TOURNAMENT

PHOENIX, MIYAZAKI

E Els	68	69	65	69	271	Y36,000,000
V Singh	72	67	70	66	275	11,680,000
T Nakajima	66	71	71	67	275	11,680,000
B Lane	67	68	72	68	275	11,680,000
F Couples	67	69	71	68	275	11,680,000
M Ozaki	66	72	65	72	275	11,680,000
D Frost	66	72	68	71	277	6,400,000
P Mickelson	68	69	67	74	278	5,800,000
K Murota	69	71	69	70	279	4,900,000
K Takahashi	67	71	67	74	279	4,900,000
B Andrade	67	74	68	71	280	3,680,000
S Simpson	66	70	71	73	280	3,680,000
T Lehman	71	69	67	73	280	3,680,000
C Stadler	67	70	73	71	281	2,650,600
T Watanabe	69	70	69	73	281	2,650,600
I Aoki	70	67	71	73	281	2,650,600
L Mize	71	66	70	74	281	2,650,600
T Watson	65	69	72	75	281	2,650,600
C Rocca	71	73	71	67	282	2,080,000

Ernie Els picked up the biggest prize on the Japanese Tour

25-28 November

CASIO WORLD OPEN

KAIMON COURSE, IBUSUKI

T Lehman	69	69	67	69	274	Y27,000,000
P Mickelson	69	71	65	70	275	15,000,000
S Higashi	67	72	68	70	277	10,200,000
J Haeggman	67	67	73	71	278	7,200,000
T Hamilton	76	69	68	67	280	6,000,000
M Brooks	68	69	74	70	281	4,850,000
C Rocca	71	71	66	73	281	4,850,000
K Tomori	69	70	75	67	281	4,850,000
F Minoza	69	67	73	73	282	3,675,000
T Watanabe	73	71	68	70	282	3,675,000
K Clearwater	69	69	71	74	283	2,760,000
M Ozaki	70	75	67	71	283	2,760,000
K Takahashi	75	67	71	68	283	2,760,000

1993 PGA Japan Tour

TOURNAMENT · WINNERS	
Tohken Cup	H Meshiai
Imperial Open	N Serizawa
Shizuoka Open	D Ishii
Taylor Made KSB Open	T Ozaki
Descente Classic	T Nishikawa
Pocarisweat Open	S Ikeuchi
Bridgestone Aso Open	S Kawamata
Chunichi Crowns	P Senior
Fuji Sankei Classic	M Ozaki
Japan PGA Championship	M Ozaki
Pepsi Ube Tournament	S Maruyama
Mitsubishi Galant	T-C Chen
JCB Sendai Classic	Y Mizumaki
Sapporo Tokyo Open	B Jones
Yomiuri Sapporo	K Hasegawa
Mizuno Open	S Okuda
PGA Philanthropy	R Mackay
Yonex Hiroshima Open	T Odate
Nikkei Cup	S Gimson
NST Niigata Open	K Idoki
Acom International	T Hamilton
Maruman Open	F Minoza
Daiwa KBC Augusta	T-C Chen
Japan PGA Matchplay	Y Yamamoto
Suntory Open	E Itai
ANA Open	T Nakajima
Jun Classic	T Suzuki
Takai Classic	S Fujiki
Japan Open Championship	S Okuda
Asahi Beer Digest	M Ozaki
Bridgestone Open	I Shirahama
Lark Cup	H Meshiai
Daiwa International	T Watanabe
Taiheiyo Masters	G Norman
Dunlop Phoenix	E Els
Casio World Open	T Lehman
Japan Series of Golf	T Nakajima
Daikyo Open	T Maruyama

LEADING · MONEY · WINNERS		
1	Hajime Meshiai	Yen 148,718,200
2	Masashi Ozaki	144,587,000
3	Tsuneyuki Nakajima	130,842,771
4	T-C Chen	112,427,166
5	Tsukasa Watanabe	103,774,100
6	Todd Hamilton	91,496,648
7	Katsunari Takahashi	89,108,132
8	Yoshinori Mizumaki	88,390,437
9	Seiki Okuda	85,208,042
10	David Ishii	83,720,330
11	Naomichi Ozaki	60,073,657
12	Yoshitaka Yamamoto	59,538,158
13	Eiichi Itai	57,588,284
14	Frankie Minoza	58,725,252
15	Kiyoshi Murota	58,207,044
16	Tomohiro Maruyama	53,713,491
17	Hiroshi Makino	53,550,248
18	Nobuo Serizawa	52,940,794
19	Ryoken Kawagishi	49,880,518
20	Shigeki Maruyama	49,295,308
21	Brian Jones	48,702,548
22	Hirofumi Miyase	46,787,415
23	Peter Senior	45,185,788
24	Toru Suzuki	42,982,188
25	Masahiro Kuramoto	41,725,030

Hajime Meshiai

REST OF THE WORLD
THE DUBAI CREEK
CHALLENGE '93

AOKI
BALLESTEROS
ELS
FALDO

Asian & African Tours

1993 Asian Tour

TOURNAMENT	WINNERS
Hong Kong Open	B Watts
Malaysian Open	G Norquist
Indian Open	A Sher
Thailand Open	C Mann
Indonesian Open	G Webb
Philippine Open	C-T Yeh
Republic of China Open	C-H Lin
Korean Open	N-S Park
Dunlop International Open	H Meshiai

Order of Merit points

1	Brian Watts	857
2	Chang-Ting Yeh	814
3	Brandt Jobe	668
4	Chin-Sheng Hsieh	660
5	Steve Flesch	585
6	Carlos Espinosa	577
7	Anthony Gilligan	536
8	Jim Rutledge	503
9	Kevin Wentworth	502
10	Bradley King	488

1992-1993 South African Tour

TOURNAMENT	WINNERS
FNB Players Championship	E Els
Goodyear Classic	E Els
Bells Cup	V Singh
Lexington PGA Championship	M McNulty
Mount Edgecombe Trophy	R Goosen
ICL International	N Price
Philips South African Open	C Whitelaw
Hollard Royal Swazi Sun	S Pappas
South African Masters	T Johnstone

Order of Merit

1	Mark McNulty	R250,079
2	Ernie Els	222,495
3	Retief Goosen	204,289
4	Roger Wessels	128,843
5	Tony Johnstone	126,601
6	Clinton Whitelaw	119,570
7	John Bland	96,251
8	Bruce Vaughan	89,976
9	James Kingston	83,955
10	Ashley Roestoff	66,620

2 - 5 December

1993 Sun City $1M Challenge

GARY PLAYER CC, SUN CITY, BOPHUTHATSWANA

N Price	67	66	66	65	264	$1,000,000
M McNulty	71	70	68	67	276	250,000
B Langer	72	69	70	68	279	200,000
F Allem	72	70	72	66	280	175,000
N Faldo	67	73	72	69	281	150,000
C Pavin	71	70	71	73	285	125,000
E Els	76	69	69	73	287	115,000
D Frost	71	70	73	74	288	110,000
M O'Meara	74	71	70	75	290	100,000
L Janzen	76	73	75	71	295	100,000
P Stewart	75	75	72	73	295	100,000
I Woosnam	76	78	80	75	309	100,000

Nick Price enjoys the fruits of four days work

1992-1993 South African Tour Review

A thank you is owing to the golfers of Zimbabwe: they have proved that Ernie Els is human after all. Throughout 1992 the young giant swept all before him in South Africa; an irresistible, all-conquering force. Els won six events that year and scored 64s and 65s as if they were going out of fashion. He easily won the 1991-92 South African Order of Merit and began his 1992-93 campaign with back-to-back victories in the FNB Players Championship and the Goodyear Classic. Then something very strange happened – Els stopped winning. In fact, he didn't win a single tournament in South Africa in 1993. He won the Dunlop Phoenix event in Japan in November but he couldn't win at home.

At the beginning of the year, 23 year-old Els held all three of the Tour's premier titles: the South African Open, Masters and PGA championships. In a shock result, Clinton Whitelaw relieved him of the South African Open trophy. Whitelaw had been rookie of the year the previous season but few thought him ready to win the Tour's most important championship of all. Tony Johnstone won the South African Masters and Mark McNulty the PGA Championship, as well as the Order of Merit for the sixth time.

Poor Ernie? Not exactly. His win in the Dunlop Phoenix tournament was actually worth more in money terms than McNulty's total winnings for the season in South Africa.

Adding to the successes of Johnstone and McNulty, Nick Price captured the ICL International to make it a hatrick of wins for Zimbabwean golfers on the 1992-93 circuit. But all this now looks small beer compared with their dominance once the 1993-94 season got under way at the end of last year. Three regular Tour events were staged in South Africa in November and December, in addition to the Sun City Million Dollar Challenge in Bophuthatswana. The parade of winners reads: McNulty, Johnstone, Price, Johnstone. Nick Price's incredible exploits at Sun City are outlined in Chapter One but his score appears opposite – and look who just happened to finish runner-up. Come back Ernie Els... all is forgiven!

Mark McNulty

The 1993 Johnnie Walker World Championship

Christmas crackers, calypso and coconuts. For the third successive year, twenty eight of the best golfers in the world gathered at the luxurious Tryall resort near Montego Bay to contest the Johnnie Walker World Championship. It was the third week in December and, despite a massive $2.7million purse, the mood was inevitably somewhat festive.

Greg Norman was conspicuous by his absence and so a repeat of 1992's extraordinary 'Duel in Jamaica', when the Australian and Nick Faldo pulled 10 strokes clear of the field on the final day, was not possible. Faldo, who won that championship in a sudden death play-off, was back to defend

(Left) blue skies, Larry Mize. (Above) the Swede and the coconut – Jesper Parnevik cools off

his title but with his game not quite at its best there was no obvious favourite for the $550,000 first prize. A close contest was anticipated - but things certainly didn't turn out that way.

The laid-back Jamaican life style tends to bring out the best in Fred Couples, winner of the inaugural staging in 1991 and he did, in fact, go on to finish strongly on this occasion. Included among Fred's most celebrated quotes is the one, 'I rarely answer the telephone in case there's somebody at the other end'. It is just as well that American Larry Mize doesn't follow Couples' example. How's this for an important message: 'Hello, is that Larry Mize?

Greg Norman has withdrawn from the Johnnie Walker World Championship in Jamaica and we were wondering if you might like to take his place?'

Larry Mize agreed, rolled up at Montego Bay and promptly set about compiling rounds of 67-66-68-65. It gave the 1987 Masters champion (and winner of two PGA Tour events in 1993) a magnificent 18 under par total of 266 which, not surprisingly, nobody came close to matching.

For three days Mize did at least have some company at the top of the leaderboard.

Ernie Els scored a 66 in the first round for a one stroke lead over Mize and Colin Montgomerie. The young South African, who came within six inches of holing his tee shot at the 5th in that opening round, then fell back on the second day with a 73 as Australia's Steve Elkington took up the challenge. Elkington eagled the 17th en route to a 65 which tied him for the halfway lead with Mize at nine under par, three shots ahead of Montgomerie. Now it was the Australian's turn to fall back - although 'collapse' is perhaps more appropriate - as he returned a disastrous 77 in the third round. With Mize scoring a 68 it left Montgomerie carrying the proverbial baton. 'Monty' himself struggled on the front nine but came back in 31 for a 68 to finish the day three behind Mize and four ahead of third-placed Bernhard Langer.

The final day is one that Scotland's best golfer will probably want to forget. 'Monty' needed to make a fast start but instead took 40 for the front nine, allowing Mize to cruise to victory. Mize, of course, didn't just 'cruise' - he went into overdrive, scoring birdies at the 3rd, 4th, 6th, 12th, 14th and 17th to win by a massive ten stroke margin. Despite making three birdies over the final nine holes, Montgomerie was overtaken by Couples, who scored a superb last-day 64, and by Langer.

If the 1993 Johnnie Walker World Championship began as a 'Caribbean Carnival', it ended as an American procession.

16 - 19 December

JOHNNIE WALKER WORLD CHAMPIONSHIP

TRYALL, MONTEGO BAY, JAMAICA

L Mize	67	66	68	65	266	$550000
F Couples	71	69	72	64	276	300000
B Langer	71	68	69	69	277	200000
C Montgomerie	67	69	68	74	278	130000
C Strange	73	68	72	66	279	100000
B Faxon	69	69	71	72	281	87500
N Faldo	70	72	69	70	281	87500
E Els	66	73	70	73	282	75000
S Elkington	68	65	77	72	282	75000
V Singh	72	70	71	69	282	75000
F Allem	69	69	72	73	283	65000
S Torrance	73	74	67	70	284	64000
C Pavin	72	75	70	68	285	62500
G Brand Jnr	70	76	72	67	285	62500
C Rocca	71	66	74	76	287	59000
J Maggert	76	67	70	74	287	59000
S Richardson	73	71	73	70	287	59000
L Janzen	73	76	70	68	287	59000
T Kite	73	74	72	68	287	59000

American Larry Mize succeeds Fred Couples and Nick Faldo to become the third Johnnie Walker World Champion

Senior Golf Review

The world of senior golf is a divided world: in the one camp there are the players who relish the challenge of the over-50s scene – a time to renew old rivalries, to replenish the bank account etc; in the other camp are the reluctant seniors, the ones who cannot quite treat it seriously. Bob Charles, Dave Stockton and Lee Trevino fall into the first category; Jack Nicklaus and Tom Weiskopf into the latter. It was ironic then that the world's most important senior event in 1993, the US Senior Open, should have developed into a thrilling contest between Nicklaus and Weiskopf.

It took place at Cherry Hills near Denver, scene of Arnold Palmer's great victory in the 1960 US Open. These days Nicklaus and Weiskopf appear to be rather more interested in golf course design than winning major championships, but there they were at Cherry Hills, going head-to-head on the back nine, just like the Masters of 1972 and 1975. The

(Right) East meets West: Japanese cowboy Isao Aoki. (Above right) Jack Nicklaus (Snr and Jnr) at Cherry Hills in the US Senior Open

Golden Bear triumphed on those two earlier occasions and now a birdie at the 70th hole followed by two solid pars enabled him to defeat Weiskopf by a single stroke and win his second US Senior championship.

Despite playing in only a limited number of over-50s events, Nicklaus' senior record is as extraordinary as it is in character with the legend. There are four 'Senior Majors' in America and by the time he was 51½ Nicklaus had claimed a victory in each of them. By the end of 1993 he had already won six of these events in just four seasons.

The great man, however, was not a contender in the first three Senior Majors last year. Tom Shaw was a surprise winner of the first, the Tradition at Desert Mountain; Tom Wargo created an even greater shock when, as a 'mere club professional', he captured the PGA Senior Championship title in Florida, and the consistent Jim Colbert won the Senior Players Championship at Dearborn, Michigan.

The failures of Ray Floyd and Isao Aoki to win a 'big one', as many predicted they would at the start of the season, can probably be put down to the fact that both were still trying to win titles on their regular tours; Floyd, of course, was also side-tracked by the small matter of helping the US retain the Ryder Cup in England.

Away from the Majors, the US Senior Tour runs from January to December and for much of 1993 Dave Stockton and Bob Charles battled for the number one spot on the money list. Stockton, who won five events to Charles' three, eventually finished on top, although both won over $1 million. George Archer played superbly in the second half of the year, winning four times to finish third on the money list, and late in the season Lee Trevino finally regained his best form.

For much of 1993 'Super Mex' was troubled by an injury to his left thumb but in the last week of September he won the Nationwide Championship and then, a week later, added the Vantage Championship, the Tour's richest event. He even had a chance to make it three in a row the following week but three-putted the final green to lose by one.

New Zealand's Bob Charles was arguably the most successful senior of all in 1993. In addition to his outstanding season in America, he won the Senior British Open Championship at Royal Lytham, finishing a stroke ahead of Gary Player and Britain's Tommy Horton, the leading player on the now burgeoning Senior Tour in Europe.

Both Charles and Player have now won the British Senior title twice and last year's event must have revived many memories as each also won an Open Championship at Royal Lytham: Charles in 1963 and the South African in 1974. Interestingly, Tony Jacklin turns 50 this year, and he too won an Open at Lytham. And I wonder on whom we shall be investing our last peseta in the year 2007?

(Above) Bob 'King' Charles in action at Royal Lytham. (Left) Lee Trevino experienced mixed emotions during 1993

The 1993 Senior Majors

1 - 4 April

The Tradition

DESERT MOUNTAIN, SCOTTSDALE, ARIZONA

T Shaw	70	65	67	67	269	$127500
M Hill	69	68	66	67	270	74800
R Floyd	69	71	69	65	274	51000
D Douglass	69	66	69	70	274	51000
G Gilbert	67	66	69	72	274	51000
I Aoki	69	65	71	70	275	34000
A Geiberger	74	69	64	69	276	30600
T Weiskopf	68	67	69	73	277	27200
J Nicklaus	72	69	70	67	278	22950
C Coody	67	72	69	70	278	22950

15 - 18 April

PGA Senior Championship

PALM BEACH GARDENS, FLORIDA

T Wargo	69	69	67	70	275	$110000
B Crampton	74	67	69	65	275	80000
(Wargo won play-off at second extra hole)						
I Aoki	72	67	69	71	279	60000
B Charles	74	67	72	68	281	40000
T Weiskopf	73	64	72	72	281	40000
M Hill	72	71	72	67	282	30000
O Moody	72	70	71	70	283	22500
J Albus	70	68	73	72	283	22500

24 - 27th June

Ford Senior Players Championship

TPC OF MICHIGAN, DEARBORN, MICHIGAN

J Colbert	67	72	70	69	278	$180000
R Floyd	68	72	71	68	279	105600
A Geiberger	72	73	69	66	280	86400
R Thompson	68	71	70	72	280	86400
J Ferree	72	69	70	72	283	49600
I Aoki	71	69	71	72	283	49600
B Charles	66	74	70	73	283	49600
J Dent	73	75	67	69	284	36000
L Gilbert	70	76	68	70	284	36000
T Weiskopf	70	71	74	70	285	31200

8 - 11 July

US Senior Open

CHERRY HILLS, ENGLEWOOD, COLORADO

J Nicklaus	68	73	67	70	278	$135330
T Weiskopf	73	69	70	67	279	72830
K Zarley	70	71	69	70	280	42346
C C Rodriguez	67	70	75	69	281	27723
D Douglass	70	71	68	72	281	27723
M Barber	70	70	73	69	282	21289
T Aycock	72	71	73	67	283	18209
R Floyd	70	73	70	70	283	18209
L Trevino	69	73	73	69	284	15864
S Hobday	71	70	74	70	285	14268
L Ziegler	69	73	70	73	285	14268
J Colbert	69	74	72	71	286	13023

US Senior Tour Order of Merit

1	Dave Stockton	$1,175,944
2	Bob Charles	1,046,823
3	George Archer	963,124
4	Lee Trevino	956,591
5	Chi Chi Rodriguez	798,857
6	Mike Hill	798,116
7	Jim Colbert	779,889
8	Bob Murphy	768,743
9	Ray Floyd	713,168
10	Simon Hobday	670,417

22 - 25 July

Senior British Open Championship

ROYAL LYTHAM AND ST ANNES, LANCASHIRE

B Charles	73	73	71	74	291	£36650
G Player	73	74	72	73	292	18905
T Horton	73	72	73	74	292	18905
A Grubb	77	73	71	72	293	11000
J S Hirsch	73	71	74	77	295	Am
L Higgins	70	71	76	79	296	8515
B Huggett	72	73	75	76	296	8515
A Proctor	73	76	73	75	297	6600
J Fourie	72	77	75	74	298	5500
D Snell	74	78	69	78	299	4292
J-M Roca	75	72	75	77	299	4292

AMATEUR GOLF REVIEW

In the early years of the next decade different names will obviously dominate the world of golf. To gain an idea of just how different these names might be, consider the following: the two leading junior golfers in America last year were 'Tiger' Woods (who has a black father and a Thai mother) and Ted Oh, whose ancestors are Korean; the current world junior champion is a Venezuelan named Gilbert Morales and the men's European Amateur champion is a young Danish golfer called Morten Backhausen; the most impressive Australasian amateur of the past two seasons has been Philip Tataurangi, a New Zealand Maori, and the rising star of southern Africa is one Lewis Chitengwa, an 18 year-old from Harare who last year became the first black golfer to win both the Zimbabwean and South African Amateur Championships.

Great things are predicted for the 1992 US Amateur champion, Justin Leonard

A different but equally interesting scenario is that the two best players in the world could both be left-handed golfers. Phil Mickelson, who turned professional mid-way through 1992 after a brilliant amateur career, is already winning events on the American PGA Tour and is expected to become one of the leading players in the world within the next few years, while the impressive winner of the Australian Amateur Championship in 1993, 19 year-old Greg Chalmers is also left-handed. Admittedly, Chalmers has a very long way to go, but at least his parents thought to give him an appropriate first name – not that we are suggesting, mind you, that there is anything intrinsically wrong with Tiger, Ted, Gilbert or Morten!

Each of the above-mentioned amateur players – and the likes of Phil Mickelson and Ernie Els for that matter – will also have to contend with the precocious Justin Leonard, the 21 year-old Texan who won the US Amateur Championship in 1992. It was generally accepted that Leonard was the best player on either side during the 1993 Walker Cup match at Interlachen (detailed ahead).

Leonard lost his US amateur crown last year to 41 year-old John Harris but demonstrated his immense potential in the US Open at Baltusrol scoring a first round 69 in the company of Nick Faldo and Tom Kite. He went on to collect the Gold Medal, awarded to the top amateur in the championship, and won several important tournaments in America throughout 1993.

Leonard's counterpart in Great Britain would appear to be 20 year-old Iain Pyman. The Yorkshire golfer won the corresponding Silver Medal as leading amateur at Royal St George's last year – his four-round total of 281 setting a new amateur record. He also won the 1993 British Amateur Championship at Royal Portrush in Northern Ireland after a magnificent final against fellow Englishman Paul Page. Pyman and Page threw a total of 21 birdies at each other during the 36 hole final before Pyman eventually triumphed at the first play-off hole.

It being an even numbered year, 1994 will see the staging of several major amateur team events. The most historic of these is the Curtis Cup and eight of Great Britain and Ireland's best women amateurs will travel to Chattanooga at the end of July to defend a trophy won in such fine style at Hoylake in 1992. A key member of the visiting team is likely to be Scotland's Catriona Lambert, winner of the 1993 Women's Amateur Championship at Royal Lytham and St Anne's. The home side, however, will be without double US Women's Amateur champion, Vicki Goetze, who joined the professional ranks in 1993. The Americans will clearly miss her at Chattanooga and again towards the end of the year when they attempt to reclaim the World Amateur Team Championship (the Espirito Trophy) which was won two years ago by Spain.

Scotland's Catriona Lambert, winner of the 1993 British Women's Amateur Championship. (Far right) New Zealand's Philip Tataurangi

The men's biennial World Amateur Team Championship (the Eisenhower Trophy) also takes place in 1994, when the defending champions – thanks in no small part to one Philip Makaera Tataurangi – will be New Zealand.

1993 US AND BRITISH AMATEUR CHAMPIONSHIPS

24 - 30 August

US AMATEUR CHAMPIONSHIP

CHAMPIONS, HOUSTON, TEXAS

QUARTER-FINALS

J Harris beat J Leonard 2 & 1

D Ellis beat B Gay 3 & 2

B Cochran beat N Begay 3 & 2

J Curley beat D Boesel 7 & 6

SEMI-FINALS

J Harris beat B Cochran 1hole

D Ellis beat J Curley 5 & 4

FINAL

J Harris beat D Ellis 5 & 3

25 - 30 May

BRITISH AMATEUR CHAMPIONSHIP

ROYAL PORTRUSH, CO ANTRIM, N IRELAND

QUARTER-FINALS

I Pyman beat M Watson 1 hole

P Page beat P Harrington 3 & 2

N Anderson beat V Phillips 1 hole

R Russell beat D Fisher 3 & 2

SEMI-FINALS

I Pyman beat N Anderson at 22nd

P Page beat R Russell 5 & 4

FINAL

I Pyman beat P Page at 37th

Iain Pyman defeated Paul Page in a superb final at Royal Portrush

9 - 14 August

US WOMEN'S AMATEUR CHAMPIONSHIP

SAN DIEGO CC, CALIFORNIA

QUARTER-FINALS

J McGill beat I Pitman 4 & 2

S Ingram beat E Knuth 3 & 1

B Schaff beat P Pedersen 3 & 2

W Ward beat D Koyama 1 hole

SEMI-FINALS

J McGill beat B Schaff 5 & 4

S Ingram beat W Ward 1 hole

FINAL

J McGill beat S Ingram 1 hole

8 - 12 June

BRITISH WOMEN'S AMATEUR CHAMPIONSHIP

ROYAL LYTHAM, LANCASHIRE, ENGLAND

QUARTER-FINALS

C Lambert beat I Tinning 2 & 1

K Speak beat M McKenna 4 & 3

S Lambert beat K McKenna 2 & 1

J Hall beat J Moodie 2 & 1

SEMI-FINALS

C Lambert beat S Lambert at 19th

K Speak beat J Hall 2 & 1

FINAL

C Lambert beat K Speak 3 & 2

1993 Walker Cup

With Interlachen near Minnesota as the venue, something remarkable was always likely to happen in the 34th Walker Cup match between the United States and Great Britain & Ireland. Interlachen is where Bobby Jones, the greatest of all amateur golfers, won a fourth US Open title during his Grandslam year of 1930. Something remarkable? The heaviest defeat in the history of the biennial event is hardly what the visitors could have had in mind! Let us not mince words; although on the first day it was an interesting contest, on the second day is was a rout: 19-5 was the final score. Captained by Vinny Giles, and led by the likes of Jay Sigel (playing in his ninth consecutive match) and Justin Leonard and John Harris (who a week later would contest the final of the US Amateur Championship) the American team was considered to be one of the strongest amateur sides ever assembled. George MacGregor's team was certainly not lacking in individual ability but as for that other crucial factor, namely experience, the team had precious little on which to draw. Four of the American squad were aged 40-something, whereas the average age of the 10 visiting players was 21 with the oldest team member just 24. With the benefit of hindsight, it is easy to suggest that the inclusion of one or two 'older heads' among the Great Britain & Ireland ranks would have been prudent; whether it would have made much of a difference is another matter.

Things actually began quite well for the visitors. A heavy storm on the first morning caused a re-jigging of the format and it was decided that 10 singles matches should be played on day one with four foursomes followed by 10 singles on the second day. Great Britain & Ireland gained two and a half points from the first four singles and if some of its players had finished better it is just possible that they could have won each of the first five matches. All but one of the other five games, however, never looked like resulting in anything other than US victories and at the end of the day the home side led by the slightly flattering margin of 6½ - 3½.

The second day was a different story altogether. The destination of the famous old trophy was effectively decided before lunch as all four of the foursomes matches were won (three of them decisively) by the home team: 6½ - 3½ suddenly became 10½ - 3½, and with only 12½ points needed for overall victory, the result was a forgone conclusion.

On a glorious, sunny afternoon the Americans emphatically underlined their superiority in the remaining ten singles matches. It was thanks only to the two Irish members of the visiting team (Raymond Burns, who won his game, despite being 3 down with 8 to play, and Padraig Harrington, who obtained a half) that a total whitewash was avoided. Rather fittingly, it was a man from Minnesota, John Harris, who collected the winning point; rather unfortunately for Great Britain & Ireland, it happened at the conclusion of only the second match in the afternoon session.

18-19 August 1993

THE 34TH WALKER CUP

INTERLACHEN, USA

DAY ONE

SINGLES (US scores given first)

A Doyle beat I Pyman (1 hole)
D Berganio lost to M Stanford (3 & 2)
J Sigel lost to D Robertson (3 & 2)
K Mitchum halved with S Cage
T Herron beat P Harrington (1 hole)
D Yates beat P Page (2 & 1)
T Demsey beat R Russell (2 & 1)
J Leonard beat R Burns (4 & 3)
B Gay lost to V Phillips (2 & 1)
J Harris beat B Dredge (4 & 3)

DAY TWO

FOURSOMES

A Doyle & J Leonard beat I Pyman & S Cage (4 & 3)
D Berganio & T Demsey beat M Stanford & P Harrington (3 & 2)
J Sigel & K Mitchum beat B Dredge & V Phillips (3 & 2)
J Harris & T Herron beat R Russell & D Robertson (1 hole)

SINGLES:

A Doyle beat D Robertson (4 & 3)
J Harris beat I Pyman (3 & 2)
D Yates beat S Cage (2 & 1)
B Gay halved with P Harrington
J Sigel beat P Page (5 & 4)
T Herron beat V Phillips (3 & 2)
K Mitchum beat R Russell (4 & 2)
D Berganio lost to R Burns (1 hole)
T Demsey beat B Dredge (3 & 2)
J Leonard beat M Stanford (5 & 4)

MATCH RESULT

United States 19, GB & Ireland 5

(Opposite page) Interlachen: the calm after the storm. (Left) the victorious American team

6

1994
A Year to Savour

JANUARY

Following the sun: the Emirates Club in Dubai, that splendid 'European' oasis, provides the setting for this classic golfing image

A decade ago the European season began in Europe; nowadays it is difficult to know which is growing faster – golf or Europe? In January this year the European Tour visits Madeira, Morocco and Dubai. The locations are almost as diverse in America where the US Tour begins its busy schedule in California, then moves to Hawaii and Arizona. In the southern hemisphere, there's plenty of championship golf in Africa with the continuation of the 1993-94 South African Tour, and in Australasia the 1994 season commences with the New Zealand Open, The Players Championship and the Heineken Classic in Perth.

FEBRUARY

Robert Louis Stevenson described it as 'the finest meeting of land and sea in the world'... and that was in its pre-golf days

The fabulous Monterey Peninsular has become a golfers' paradise and in February thousands will make their annual pilgrimage to the Pebble Beach Pro-Am, one of the most popular events on the US circuit. Australian Brett Ogle scored a memorable first American victory here in 1993. Meanwhile, Down Under, the highlight of the month is the Australian Masters at Huntingdale. The South African Tour winds down in February but the Asian Tour starts up and immediately brushes shoulders with the European Tour which stages the Johnnie Walker Classic in Phuket, Thailand.

MARCH

The first Major of 1994 will be staged here: Mission Hills, near Palm Springs, home to the Nabisco Dinah Shore tournament, which is recognised as 'the Masters of women's golf'

Last year, Helen Alfredsson (inset), became the second Swedish player to win one of the LPGA's major championships, following Lotte Neumann's great success in the 1988 US Women's Open. Florida provides the principal focus for men's golf with the prestigious Players Championship being staged at Sawgrass. In Europe the Tour cruises around the Mediterr-anean hosting events in Spain, Portugal and Italy.

APRIL

Golfers and caddies, green carpets and Green Jackets. Nick Faldo and Payne Stewart walk along one of Augusta National's famous velvet fairways during last year's Masters

Faldo and Stewart are likely to start as two of the favourites for the 58th Masters in April. Seven of the last 11 coveted Green Jackets have been claimed by European golfers but the biggest threats to a home success may come from Nick Price of Zimbabwe, who led the US money list in 1993 and Australian Greg Norman, the reigning British Open champion. Across the water in Europe the Pals Golf Club in Girona is the venue for the 1994 Heineken Open Catalonia.

MAY

**Will May see the re-emergence of the matador?
It is the month of the Spanish Open and with spring finally embracing Britain, Seve will likely visit the land of his greatest triumphs**

Two European Tour events will be held in England in May, the Benson and Hedges International at St Mellion and the Volvo PGA Championship at Wentworth; Seve has never won the former (although his fellow Spaniard, Olazabal did in 1990) but he has twice won the latter, and his victory in 1991 set him up for a vintage season. As well as the Spanish Open, May brings the Italian Open and in America the most important tournaments are the Memorial and Colonial events on the PGA Tour and the McDonald's LPGA Championship in Wilmington, Delaware.

JUNE

A classic American golf course in a tranquil Irish setting: the Jack Nicklaus-designed course at Mount Juliet is widely acknowledged as one of the finest new courses in Europe

Mount Juliet hosts its second Murphy's Irish Open at the end of the month, Nick Faldo having won his third successive Irish championship there last year. In America, during the same week, Nick Price is expected to put up a strong defence at the Western Open and a fortnight prior to that perhaps one of the two 'great Nicks' will end the American golfers' monopoly of their national championship; Lee Janzen (left) defends at Oakmont.

JULY

After Nicklaus v Watson in 1977 came the 'Norman conquest' of 1986; the 1994 Open Championship at Turnberry has much to live up to

But how could an Open at Turnberry ever be dull? The Ailsa Course is the most scenic on the championship rota and although Nicklaus, Watson and Norman produced some astonishing scores, if the wind blows, the ghost of Robert the Bruce may have the last laugh. One week before Turnberry, Gleneagles stages the Bell's Scottish Open and immediately after the British Open comes the Heineken Dutch Open at Hilversum. The US Tour maintains a fairly low profile in July but elsewhere Great Britain and Ireland defend the Curtis Cup and both the Senior and LPGA Tours stage their version of the US Open.

AUGUST

'Don't hurry, don't worry and be sure to smell the flowers along the way.' Costantino Rocca follows Ian Woosnam's tee shot at the Murphy's English Open last August

For 36 holes the mighty Welshman and the mighty Italian locked horns in a thrilling head to head confrontation with Woosnam shooting 65-66 and Rocca 64-69. As well as an English Open, August also sees a British Open – the Weetabix Women's British Open at Woburn where Australian Karen Lunn will be defending champion. In America, Southern Hills, Tulsa, Oklahoma, is the venue for the 76th USPGA Championship and if the event is half as exciting as the 1993 championship at Inverness it will be worth watching. The year's final Major is followed by The International at Castle Pines and the World Series at Firestone.

SEPTEMBER

Alpine golf. The course at Crans-sur-Sierre in Switzerland must rank among the most photogenic in the world; each year it hosts the Canon European Masters

Golfing miracles also happen there: in last year's tournament Seve Ballesteros manufactured an 'impossible' approach to the 18th green (see chapter one) and in 1992 Jamie Spence produced a final round of 60 to claim his first ever European title. September is not the same without a Ryder Cup but there are still plenty of big events in Europe including the Lancôme Trophy, the British Masters and the European Open and on the US Tour there is the Canadian Open at Glen Abbey, won last year by David Frost.

October

Will they still be smiling come October? Europe's women golfers achieved a shock victory in the 1992 Solheim Cup at Dalmahoy: winning in America may prove more difficult

The Greenbrier, West Virginia is the venue for the eagerly awaited 3rd Solheim Cup encounter. October is Autumn and that means the World Matchplay Championship at Wentworth and the Alfred Dunhill Cup at St Andrews. It also sees the climax of both the European and US circuits with the Volvo Masters and Tour Championship events; Autumn in Europe ('Fall' in America) but Spring in the southern hemisphere as championship golf recommences in Australasia, and in Japan, October brings the Japan Open.

NOVEMBER

Puerto Rican paradise: two-by-two, the golfing nations of the world will be descending upon Dorado Beach in November for the 40th Heineken World Cup

The beautifully situated 18th green on the Championship East Course is pictured above. Can 'Uncle Sam' make it three wins in a row? And will an American golfer emulate Brad Faxon's triumph (inset) by winning the Heineken Australian Open at Royal Sydney later in the month. Although the domestic seasons in Europe and America may be over, there remains much to play for in Australasia, Japan and southern Africa

DECEMBER

Heavens above! Nick Price has just holed his second shot for an eagle at the 1st during the final round of the 1993 Million Dollar Challenge in Sun City

As well as being a star in Africa, the popular Zimbabwean was also last year's leading moneywinner (worldwide) and Player of the Year in America. Price will probably spend much of December playing the South African Tour but there are important tournaments too in Japan and Australia as their 1994 seasons draw to a close. Elsewhere in the world, however, the focus shifts to Skins Games, Shoot Outs and jackpots in Jamaica.

1994 Majors

A preview by Matthew Chancellor

They are the most important days of the year. The world's leading players plan their calendars around them. And uniquely, in today's multi-million-dollar game, they do not, nor ever will, pay appearance money. They are the four major championships, the Masters, the US Open, the Open and the USPGA.

'This will change your life', Payne Stewart told Wayne Grady in 1990 when he handed over his USPGA crown to the Australian. When Ian Baker-Finch won his Open Championship at Birkdale the following year, he found himself spending an extra hour a day signing autographs. And even a reticent Tom Kite, who had spent the best part of 20 years playing down their importance, was forced to concede after his own 1992 US

No tournament is more eagerly awaited than The Masters and no course possesses greater appeal than Augusta

Open triumph: 'I never quite realised the kind of attention I would get.'

They are the yardstick by which history judges every player. It is Jack Nicklaus' haul of 18 professional majors that singles him out as the game's supreme competitor. It is Ben Hogan's 1953 triple slam, when he won the Masters, US Open and Open Championship in the space of a few months, that adds the extra glory to the legend of the man with the perfect swing. And despite his many millions, it is Greg Norman's haul of only two majors in his career thus far, that prevents the supremely talented Aussie from joining the greats at the pinnacle of the game.

Golf's four majors are the rhythms by which the pulse of every new golfing season takes its beat. Each is uniquely different. The beauty of the Masters gives way to the severity of the US Open. The history and grandeur of an Open Championship leads into the heat and surprise of a USPGA.

For many the season does not begin until April and the Masters. The Masters is Augusta National. And Augusta National is Bobby Jones. The course he helped create remains a living memorial to the greatest amateur golfer the game has ever seen.

This year's tournament, April 7-10, marks the 60th anniversary of Jones' 'little invitational' as it was when he invited a few old friends to his course in 1934. They came in homage to see Jones, and to see how he and Alister Mackenzie had transformed the old fruit plantation that had stood there.

Although the youngest of the four majors, for many it is the most eagerly anticipated. As he slipped his arms into his second Green Jacket last year Bernhard Langer declared: 'This is the best tournament in the world.' Well, as it is the only major Langer has so far won, you might say, 'he would say that wouldn't he?' It is probably the easiest major to win. Its limited 80-odd-man field includes a generous helping of ageing champions and youthful amateurs, none of whom harbour any real prospect of winning. The hardest part is getting an invitation in the first place.

That the Masters Green Jackets have become one of the most prized rewards in golf, has much to do with the course that their winners must master. Augusta National, with its blazing shrubs and colour is one of the most supremely beautiful courses in the world. But

Ernie Els – 'a major champion waiting to happen'

it is as deadly as it is lovely. Augusta's back nine are among the most memorable holes in the world. Amen Corner, the stretch from the 11th through to the 13th, is probably the most famous necklace of holes anywhere. Water comes treacherously into play at each, and a player who contends at Augusta, puts his heart and hopes in his mouth each time he stands on the 11th tee.

While the season's first major has been kind to Europe – seven of the last 11 Masters have been won by European golfers – the US Open has remained almost permanently wrapped in the stars and stripes of Uncle Sam. Since the Second World War there have been only three foreign winners: Gary Player in 1965, Tony Jacklin in 1970 and David Graham in 1981.

While the Masters is synonymous with wide, encouraging fairways and welcoming greens, the US Open clings to its fierce reputation for narrow fairways fringed by jungle-rough and rock hard greens. Champions rarely win US Opens, they survive them. As Nick Faldo memorably put it after Tom Kite's victory at Pebble Beach in 1992: 'The USGA screwed everyone here except Tom Kite. The score is Tom Kite 1, USGA 149.'

Faldo does not bother to hide how badly he wants a US Open. Despite three British Opens and two Masters titles, he needs a US Open for his place to be secure among the game's true greats. Indeed, although the Englishman's precision game of hitting fairways and greens is ideally suited to the tournament's demands, a play-off defeat to Curtis Strange in 1988 is the nearest Faldo has come so far.

This year's US Open, June 16-19, returns for the seventh time to Oakmont Country Club in Pennsylvania. Past US Open champions there include Ben Hogan in his triple slam year of 1953, and Jack Nicklaus a decade later when he won the first of his four championships. As well as hosting triumphs by two of the game's greatest ever players, it was also the back-drop to what has been called the greatest ever round of golf.

In 1973 Johnny Miller won his only US Open at Oakmont by shooting a final round

(Left) the famous 'church pews' bunker at Oakmont; (below) Jack Nicklaus congratulates Tom Watson after their 1977 'Duel in the Sun' at Turnberry

63, eight under par. At the time it was the lowest round ever in a major, and, though it has since been equalled, it remains unsurpassed.

While US Open courses are infamous for their fairway rough, Oakmont's reputation rests upon its bunkers – all 220-odd of them. They are both plentiful and, when you are in them, extravagant. The course boasts one of the most famous sand traps in golf – the church pews. This vast bunker, which comes into play both on the 3rd and 4th holes, owes its clerical name to its appearance. A row of grassy banks slice it from front to back.

From the waiting traps of Oakmont it is on to the pot bunkers of the Open. And whatever his exploits thus far in 1994, this year's Open Championship, July 14-17, will inevitably be concerned with the fortune of Greg Norman.

The reigning champion returns to defend his Claret Jug in, of all places, Turnberry, at the course where he won his first, and only other major in 1986. In dreadful windy conditions, Norman was the only player to shoot level par, wining by five shots from his nearest challenger. Victory was built upon a record-equalling second round 63, which

Turnberry's Ailsa Course enjoys an incomparable setting

included a three-putt at the last from 28 feet.

The win was supposed to open a flood-gate of opportunities to the blond Australian. What followed, however, is a well-known tale of unparalleled misfortunes. It is one of the quirky ironies of fate, however, that Norman returns to the scene of his first great triumph, both as a champion and as golf's great, battered survivor.

Next year's Open may be the 123rd playing, but it will be only the third time it has visited Turnberry's Ailsa Course. Resting beside the glittering water of the Firth of Clyde, this spectacular links is arguably the most beautiful stop on the Open rota – especially when the sun shines, which has been known to happen, and when it sets. And with the isle of Arran towering to the north-west, the massive volcanic eruption called Ailsa Craig standing imperious to the south, and its famous lighthouse, Turnberry's landmarks are already icons of the modern game.

Its Open history may be short, but Turnberry can boast arguably the greatest Open of them all. In their famous 'Duel in the Sun', two of the finest players the game will ever see, Jack Nicklaus and Tom Watson, turned the first Turnberry Open into a closed show. Nicklaus' 269 total would have won him the championship in every previous year; in 1977, however, it was only good enough for a runner-up spot behind Watson's 268 – the remainder of the field finished at least 10 behind Nicklaus.

Be it a British Open, Masters or US Open, it is a golfing cliché that no-one ever wins without driving the ball well. This will be especially true at Southern Hills, venue of this year's USPGA Championship, August 11-14.

As much as any course in the world, Southern Hills is made for driving specialists, that is those who can hit the ball long, and straight. A par 70 of nearly 7,000 yards, the course has become renowned for its tight, narrow fairways, as well as a par five, the 5th, of 630 yards. Problems off the tee are further magnified by the tendency to grow the Bermuda grass to fearsome heights whenever a championship is held there.

The 1958 US Open at Southern Hills, won by Tommy Bolt, is remembered for the infamous rough and blistering heat that week. Ben Hogan withdrew from the tournament after straining his wrist trying to escape from the rough. Bolt played magnificently, missing only 13 of the 72 greens in regulation – and he still finished at three over. The runner-up was Gary Player, seven over, who admitted to playing some of the best golf of his career.

This year the refined country club at Tulsa in Oklahoma, hosts its third USPGA to go with two US Opens. It is a proud and honourable record for a club that was born out of the American depression. The story is told how in 1935 an oil millionaire agreed to donate 300 acres of land for a course, as long as the club members came up with $150,000 to build it. The money had to be found in 18 days and incredibly, it was, with one day to spare. It is a sobering thought that at this year's USPGA the golfing millionaires will be playing for over 10 times as much as the course cost to build.

But it is not for the money that the best gather together for four weeks each year. It is for the glory. Bobby Jones, who won four US Opens, three British Opens, five US Amateur titles, and one British Amateur – in 1930 when he completed the unique Grand Slam of all four in the same year – defined the essence of a major championship. 'There are,' said the gentleman amateur, 'tournament winners, and *major* tournament winners.'

Jones' distinction remains as true as ever.

1994 Major Championship Dates

April 7-10: The Masters
June 16-19: The US Open
July 14-17: The Open Championship
August 11-14: The USPGA

Nick Faldo will be seeking to add to his collection of five major titles in 1994 – no player will be better prepared

1994 Heineken World of Golf

A Preview by Richard Dyson

For the second year running Heineken's substantial commitment to the world of golf includes the sponsorship of five top men's professional events. As widespread in terms of the golfing calendar (running from January to November) as it is in a geographical sense (commencing and concluding in Australia via Spain, Holland and Puerto Rico), this year's Heineken World of Golf programme follows the formula so successfully established in 1993 and promises to be every bit as enthralling.

The schedule begins in late January with the Heineken Classic at the lavish Vines Resort in the Swan Valley – a wine connoisseur's dream setting near Perth. The Vines is one of a number of major developments, such as Sanctuary Cove and Coolum, which have sprung up in recent years and added greatly to the burgeoning golfing scene Down Under by staging events on the Australasian Tour.

Formerly known as The Vines Classic, the title followed the local wines into export in 1990 and 1991 when Americans Jeff Maggert and Blaine McCallister were the respective champions. Home-grown produce reasserted itself in 1992, in the appropriate form of wine enthusiast Ian Baker-Finch, while last year, the

Fred Couples in action at Lake Nona during the 1993 Heineken World Cup; in 1994 the event will be staged at Dorado Beach in Puerto Rico

first of Heineken sponsorship, Peter Senior produced a vintage performance. In sizzling temperatures, Senior swept to a three stroke victory over a quality field (which included Aussie Major men; Baker-Finch, Grady and Norman) as his now familiar broomstick putter 'caught fire'. With strong support from Western Australian golf fans (record galleries of 43,000 attended in 1993) and another top class entry expected to assemble at this demanding but highly popular lay-out, the Heineken Classic success story looks set to continue in 1994.

The Heineken Open Catalonia, like the Heineken Classic, is a tournament with a short history but one which is increasing in prestige every year. First staged in 1989, as the Catalan Open, it provided a first Tour win for England's Mark Roe, then, after lapsing for a year, home victories followed for Señors Rivero and Olazabal. Last year, when Heineken became title sponsors, the event was moved back from mid March to late April and staged at the Osona Montanya Golf Club, which is situated in the mountains 30 miles north east of Barcelona. A consequence of such a location can be adverse climatic conditions and last year after a rain-delayed third round, snow, hail, thunder and lightning forced the final round to be abandoned. Scotland's Sam Torrance, thanks largely to a brilliant course record 63 on day two, thus claimed a 3-day victory which drew inevitable comparisons with the Olympic equestrian 3-day event which the club had staged the previous year. In 1994 the Heineken Open Catalonia moves

Sam Torrance leads the way during the 1993 Heineken Open Catalonia

Colin Montgomerie – Europe's number one in 1993 and the Heineken Dutch Open champion

back towards the coast to Girona and the impressive Golf Club de Pals. Famed for its wealth of umbrella pines, the course was the venue for the 1972 Spanish Open and, more recently, the 1991 Girona Open won by Steven Richardson.

Snow and hail should never be a problem at the Heineken Dutch Open, which retains its established place following the Open Championship in late July and always boasts a high-calibre international entry. This is clearly reflected by the quality of the last three champions: Payne Stewart, Bernhard Langer and Colin Montgomerie. These three championships were all played over the majestic Noordwijkse links, but this year the event heads inland to Hilversum, an attractive tree-lined course 15 miles south east of Amsterdam.

The Dutch Open has a history dating back

to 1919 and Hilversum, which first hosted the event in 1923, has staged it 13 times – the last seeing victory for Welshman Mark Mouland in 1988. It was at Hilversum in 1936 that Belgium's Flory van Donck won the first of his five Dutch Open titles – two more than, amongst other people, Seve Ballesteros, winner at the club in 1980. Seve, for whom the 1976 Dutch Open provided his first PGA European Tour success, will always have a soft spot for the event and so too will Colin Montgomerie after his victory last year ended a near two-year barren spell. 'Monty' was laughing all the way to the bank after claiming 'a nice little earner' of £108,330 (£8,330 more than Greg Norman's Open cheque) – obviously a case of Heineken refreshing the winning instincts other tournaments couldn't reach!

Trees will replace sandhills when the Heineken Dutch Open moves inland in 1994

A toast was most certainly drunk at last year's Heineken World Cup by the Puerto Rican delegation after it was announced that Dorado Beach will stage the 40th playing of the prestigious team event this November; in so doing it will become only the fifth venue to have hosted the tournament more than once. Dorado staged the 1961 Canada Cup (as it was known from its inception in 1953 until 1966) and fittingly, considering the Caribbean island's allegiance to America, 'Uncle Sam' stole the show or to be more precise 'Slammin' Sam' did. Sam Snead, with a superb 272 (-16) aggregate ran away with the International Trophy by eight strokes and teamed up with Jimmy Demaret to win team honours by 12 strokes. At the time the Americans had a combined age of 99 so it seems appropriate that Dorado has recently been the venue for the season-ending Tour Championship on the US Senior Tour – the very stage upon which Chi Chi Rodriquez, 'Mr Puerto Rican Golf' has had such success in recent times.

The 1994 Heineken World Cup will be staged over the Championship East course at this idyllic coastal complex, east of San Juan. Carved from a swamp by the legendary Robert Trent Jones, it was incomplete in 1961 when the event was held over a composite course. The adjacent Atlantic Ocean, whose breezes will be so influential, is not the only water factor, for numerous small lakes also lie in wait for errant competitors.

The World Cup has done a great deal to fulfil its aim of international goodwill through golf, despite US domination (with 19 team and 14 individual wins), countries from all six continents have won both titles and there have been many surprise winners. There were no surprises last year though, at majestic Lake Nona, as America's Fred Couples and Davis Love became only the second partnership (after Nicklaus and Palmer) to successfully defend the team title with a display of quite superb golf. A third consecutive win would be unprecedented. Bernhard Langer, so impressive in taking the International Trophy for the first time will no doubt be aware that only Jack Nicklaus has ever successfully defended it.

(Top) The 11th hole at Dorado Beach (East Course); (above) Bernhard Langer

The final chapter of Heineken's own 'Famous Five' series will be written in late November when the most important event on the Australasian Tour, the Heineken Australian Open is staged at Royal Sydney. This famous club celebrated its centenary last year and from humble beginnings has developed into a vast sporting complex. Set in a large natural bowl amid fashionable Sydney suburbs, the course has an abundance of trees but also the feel of a links about it and, being close to the sea, is subject to the full vagaries of the wind. It will be the tenth time that it has staged the Australian Open, the first being in 1906 and

The 18th at Royal Sydney, venue of the 1994 Heineken Australian Open

the last in 1988, when American Mark Calcavecchia claimed a six stroke victory with a sensational 269 (-19) total. Other post war winners at the club have been Ossie Pickworth, Bruce Crampton and record seven-time Australian Open champion, Gary Player.

This year's Australian Open, the third to be sponsored by Heineken, is special because it is the championship's 90th Anniversary year. Defending champion at Royal Sydney will be Brad Faxon, who joined a growing list of recent US winners last year at Metropolitan when inspired putting gave him a two stroke victory. Indeed, Americans together with Australians have completely dominated the event of late; the last 19 championships having yielded 11 home victories and eight US successes.

Royal Sydney boasts one of the game's finest closing holes, a demanding 410-yards uphill par four which dog-legs left around trees to reach a large, well bunkered green backed by the imposing clubhouse. No finer setting could be wished for to bring down the curtain on the Heineken year.

1994 Heineken World of Golf Dates

Jan 27-30:	Heineken Classic
April 21-24:	Heineken Open Catalonia
July 21-24:	Heineken Dutch Open
Nov 10-13:	Heineken World Cup Golf
Nov 24-27:	Heineken Australian Open

Robert Allenby

Pine Valley, New Jersey is often ranked as the best golf course in the world

7

Great Golf Courses of the World

The New and the Old, Down Under: (main picture) the 19th hole at Paradise Palms, a dazzling new course situated north of Cairns in Queensland; (inset) Royal Melbourne is still regarded as the greatest course in the southern hemisphere

...and there are still those who claim that golf is bad for the environment: San Roque in southern Spain (left) and Desert Mountain in Arizona (above) provide two fine examples of how golf can transform a barren landscape

(Above) South Africa's latest diamond: The Lost City Golf Club at Sun City, Bophuthatswana. (Left) An Augusta in Japan: the Taiheiyo Club, home of the prestigious Japanese Masters tournament

Two of the newest, toughest and prettiest finishes in England: (top) the 18th on the East Course at East Sussex National; (above) the closing hole at Castle Combe in Wiltshire

(Left) Golfing treasure: Spyglass Hill, a next-door neighbour to Cypress Point and Pebble Beach, owes its name to the imagination of RL Stevenson.

(Above) Royal Dornoch has been described by Tom Watson as 'one of the great courses of the five continents'. It is the most northerly situated of Scotland's famous championship links and, before the likes of Tom Watson discovered its charms, it enjoyed a splendid isolation. Ballyliffin (left) looks set to become the 'Dornoch of Ireland'. Located close to Malin Head in the far north of Donegal, its setting is genuinely captivating and the links terrain so pure that Nick Faldo described it as 'one of the most natural courses I have ever seen.'